Each Night, I Die

Each Night, I Die

Reload

David Belton

Each Night, I Die
Copyright © 2018 by David Belton. All rights reserved.

No part of this publication may be reproduced, stored in a retrieval system or transmitted in any way by any means, electronic, mechanical, photocopy, recording or otherwise without the prior permission of the author except as provided by USA copyright law.

The opinions expressed by the author are not necessarily those of Stonewall Press.

Published in the United States of America

ISBN: 978-1-949362-97-8 (*sc*)
    978-1-949362-96-1 (*e*)

Library of Congress Control Number: 2018957031

Published by Stonewall Press
4800 Hampden Lane, Suite 200, Bethesda, MD 20814 USA
1.888.334.0980 | www.stonewallpress.com

1. Memoirs (Biography/Autobiography)
18.10.10

In loving memory of my beloved mother, Bernice Belton, who departed this life on December 30, 2006, but lives in my heart forever.

To my daughter, LaSharon Belton; my sister, Daisy Belton; and to my brother, Alton Carter; you have inspired me beyond words.

Contents

Acknowledgments 9
Prelude 11

   1   Death of Souls 15
   2   Summer of '85 33
   3   Picking Up The Pieces 39
   4   Going Astray 49
   5   Another Chance 59
   6   Home Again 71
   7   The Promised Land 81
   8   Going Nowhere Fast 97
   9   Too Far To Turn Back 113
  10   Out of Control 125
  11   954 Forrest Street 133
  12   We Almost Made It 143
  13   The Resurrection 161
  14   The Morning After 175
  15   The Long Ride Back 187
  16   Redemption 217

A Personal Letter To My Daughter 245
About The Author 249

Acknowledgments

TIME AND SPACE WILL not permit me to acknowledge all those who have supported me throughout this long journey, but I would be remiss if I failed to recognize a few individuals for their support, prayers, and inspiration.

To Ladell Muhammad, who was there when I embarked upon this long odyssey, I express my sincere gratitude, and it's doubtful if I would have pursued higher education had it not been for her.

To Pastor Nancy Engen, my mentor and spiritual mom, you were a godsend, and I am grateful to have been a beneficiary of the Alpha & Omega Prison Ministry.

To my dear friend, Mark Rowley, I am grateful you were there to give me that needed nudge when I wandered off course.

To the Community Correction Service Committee Prison Volunteers, thanks for your time and service you gave unselfishly, to the least of those marginalized and left to wither and die on the side of the road.

To Larry Gaither, David Manley, Aunt Flossie, John Wormley Jr., Ahmad Noroozi, and Johnathan McFadden, for your kindness and generosity, I'm deeply appreciative.

Finally, to my church family FBCG and men focus groups, what can I say? You were exactly what I needed when I was on the verge of losing my way. Because of you, I learned the value of being in small groups. As Dr. Johnny Parker often stated, "A man can't know himself, grow himself, by himself." And you gave me a safe place to be transparent.

Prelude

I SAW HER PICK up the phone; she held it to her ear for only a minute, and the receiver fell to the floor. I looked at her in a state of shock. Paralyzed, I watched her open her mouth wide as if she tried to scream, yet no sound escaped. She was paralyzed and unable to move, and her mouth was still wide open. Suddenly she fell to her knees as if the weight of her body was too heavy. She began to swing and fight the air with her small fist and tears ran like a flood from her eyes. She shook her head from side to side in disbelief as if what she had just heard would soon go away. When her voice returned, all I heard her say was one word.

"No! No!" Again and again she screamed.

I felt a ball of tension burning inside my chest. I tried to shut out the sight and sound of a reality that was too much for even me to bear. No one had to tell me that he was dead. Chest was gone forever; that was the meaning of it all. My nephews had lost a father; my sister had lost a loving companion, and I had lost a dear friend.

I never realized how uncertain life could be. I should have, but I didn't. Suddenly I felt like an old man, and all I wanted to do was forget. Why did life have to be this way? Why did the good have to die so young? Why did the world have to be this way? For some reason, I was always running, never stopping long enough to see what was important or real. I was always running, trying to cross an imaginary finish line and looking for the real Promised Land. My inner struggles and conflicts made me a prisoner of my own inner hell. One day I woke up and realized that there was no finish line; there was no real Promised Land, and the dream I lived existed nowhere else but in my drug crazed head.

On October 7, 1985, behind the dismal and gloomy walls of the Maryland Penitentiary, I surrendered my life to God. I had a genuine, religious experience that completely changed my life forever; a thousand nights I had to die, to one day die no more.

David Belton

DEATH OF SOULS

When you have lost everything in this world
you have ever loved.
When you are marched away in chains
not justly,
But because of games, ignorance and illusions.

When darkness falls and your soul dies,
A thousand deaths between dust and dawn,
When you cry blood instead of tears,
And the hurt and torment cuts so deep
That you just want to lie down and die.

When your burdens become so severe,
More than flesh and blood can bear,
This I call the death of souls,
A hell unlike no other.

1

Death of Souls

"Black men born in the U.S. and fortunate enough to live past the age of eighteen are conditioned to accept the inevitability of prison..."

George Jackson, 1970

I THOUGHT ABOUT THESE words that Brother George had written as I was taking another free ride down 1-95 against my will. Again, I had become another statistic of the Department of Correction recidivism. Then I wondered what this black Prince would have said if he had lived long enough to see America become the world's leader with the highest percentage of its population locked behind bars, with black men incarcerated at a rate four times that of South Africa.

When I was much younger, I had dreams of becoming a freedom fighter, fighting for the liberation of black folks. But somehow along the way I got sidetracked, and instead, I became a criminal. Without realizing it, I had become programmed for life. I had become programmed towards the pig trough, and I didn't know how to get out of it because I thought the whole world was a pig pen. So many thoughts flooded my mind as I traveled toward my destination, Lorton Reformatory; it was located about twenty miles south of Washington, D.C. Convicted felons who were not transferred to federal prisons went to Lorton. However, because Washington is a federal city, many convicts were later transferred out to federal prisons.

It was 1973, and I had been sentenced to nine months for CDW (carrying a dangerous weapon). At Lorton, there were more familiar faces; I saw faces I hadn't seen in many years. Once there, I had to stay behind the wall for thirty days during orientation. "Behind the wall" was really a prison within a prison. Primarily, it housed the most dangerous convicts and those with disciplinary problems and those awaiting transfer to federal penitentiaries. All of the facilities the general population had were behind the wall. They had a visiting room, dining room, hospital, a huge recreation yard, small work details, etc.

All incoming convicts were placed in a cell block with four men to a cell. I was assigned to a cell with my old con partner, Calcutta. Later, they put two very young guys in our cell who were friends of Softy. One of the young brother's name was John Henry. One afternoon when we were walking the yard, one of the younger guys in our cell asked John Henry, "When is the last time you heard anything about Softy?"

John Henry looked at him and said, "You should ask his brother." Then looked at me and smiled.

The youngster was dumbfounded; he was puzzled. Then it dawned on him. "Cheese, are you and Softy brothers?"

"All our lives," I said. And we all burst into laughter.

"Cheese, he is good as gold, but he is a madman if I've ever seen one." We all laughed again because we all knew he had spoken the absolute truth. The three of them had been in training school together, but he would never have guessed Softy and I were brothers.

"Hey Cal," I asked, "whatever happened to Katie?"

"The last time I saw her she was living with Tank," Cal answered.

"He's a fool, and he won't hold her long. I just hate to see a chump dog a good woman."

"Cheese, why don't you tell John the real reason you don't like Tank," Cal said.

"Why don't you like him?" John asked.

Before I could answer, Cal said, "Tank hit on Jean a few years ago and Cheese kicked all the sparks out of his butt."

"The fool is lucky I didn't kill him," I said. Jean was my woman and later became the mother of my kids.

"You probably would have if it hadn't been for her. At times you can be just as crazy as Softy," Cal said.

After thirty days, I went into population with approximately ten other convicts. We boarded a green bus from behind the wall and rode slowly through the gigantic compound; it was enormous. Lorton was the largest prison I had ever been in. It was set on hundreds of acres and reminded me of a small city. Behind the wall, there were only cell blocks, but on the compound, there was nothing but dormitories. There were 25 dorms scattered over the many acres divided into large and small dorms.

When the bus stopped beside the captain's office, a crowd of convicts were standing around to see who got off. Many cons lost their lives as soon as they stepped off this bus. Several were actually killed on the spot. They stuck up the wrong dealers on the street. They had old grudges and unsettled disputes. But the worst offense you could commit against another con was to get too sweet with his lady while he was incarcerated.

A small group was waiting for me when I got off the bus, and I was really glad to see them. There were no guards to take you by the hand and babysit you. They told you where to get a mattress and where your dorm was located, and you were on your own. When I got my mattress and found an empty bunk in the dorm, it was just like homecoming. All my friends were here: Fats, Sammy, Nae, Scrooge, Thin-man, Cowboy and a host of others. I also met new friends: Pimping Slim, Rabbit, Hatchett-Bey, and a few more.

On one hand, Lorton was dangerous. It was so dangerous when I arrived that the guards made jokes about it being the combat zone. There were so many murders that I lost count. Even a prison guard was killed during the short while I was there. The only time the guards came into the dorms was to make count or a shake-down.

On the other hand, it was considered by many to be one of the best prisons in the United States in which to serve time. It could easily make you forget where you were, and many did. There was a wide variety of outside activities and always something to do. You could stay out on the compound until 11 p.m. every night. Then everyone had to report to his assigned dorm. Many had jobs in the city. They would leave for work early in the morning and not return until 10 p.m. Also, some were released five days a week to attend the college program.

After I was in Lorton for a short time, the state of Maryland placed a detainer on me for Murder-1 and shortly thereafter the Maryland court began their procedures. All my friends were aware that I had an M-1 in Maryland, and they gave me jailhouse legal advice on how to beat my case. When my attorney arrived to visit from Maryland, all he had was bad news. The State had the signed statement of three co-defendants who said I planned and committed the murder. I had everything against me and nothing in my favor. The State's attorney was willing to drop the M-1 to second degree if I pled guilty, but that was out of the question. Second degree murder carried a penalty of 30-years; how could I plead guilty to a 30-year prison sentence? I could tell he didn't want to go to trial. He wanted the easy way out, but I told him I would take my chance with a jury.

Late one evening the guards informed me that I was going to court the following morning. When I asked the reason, no one seemed to know. All they could tell me was that it was P.G. County.

Early the next morning I was heavily bound with chains and put in a van. We stopped behind the wall and picked up another convict. It was one of the Awkward Brothers. He had escaped from the D.C. Jail with Mace Brown, Roach Henry, Cadillac Smith and seven others. While on escape he was charged with murder in P.G. County. We were transported to the District Court and then to P.G. County by federal marshals.

The marshals told us that we were going for an arraignment. It was to be brief. We were marched into the courthouse heavily guarded. It was like we were spectacles in a circus or freaks in a sideshow. We were looked upon with eyes of contempt, scorn, and fear. We were looked upon like we were wild animals who had gone mad, and now everyone had come to witness our death so they could all applaud and say amen.

It was not for an arraignment; it was a bond hearing. The judge called awkward first.

"Young man, do you have money to make bond?"

"No, I don't, your Honor." His face was dead serious, and the courtroom became extremely quiet. "I don't have any money, property or collateral. And the reason I don't have anything is because your people promised my people 40 acres and a mule, and we haven't got that yet." The courtroom burst into laughter, but the judge didn't think it was amusing. He set a very high and outrageous bond and a date for arraignment.

It was a necessary procedure according to the law, but it meant nothing to us. Neither of us could go anywhere because we were serving other sentences. My bond was set at $100,000 and a hearing for November. Then we were rushed back to Lorton.

While I was in Lorton, I really didn't prepare for the fight. I kept procrastinating. I kept saying tomorrow, tomorrow, I'll do it tomorrow. But tomorrow for me never came.

Softy was raising so much hell that my mother had to bring him down one afternoon so I could try to talk to him. But what on earth could I tell him? I was many years too late, and I knew there was nothing I could do. But still, I had to try.

When I entered the visiting room and saw him along with mom, I was shocked; I couldn't believe it. This was the first time he had come to see me in prison, and it had nothing to do with love; it was all about superstition. He was the most superstitious person I had ever known. If a black cat crossed his path, if you swept his feet with a broom, if he broke a mirror, to be the third person to light his cigarette from the same match, to walk underneath a ladder, bad dreams, he associated all these crazy things with bad luck. He even considered visiting anyone in prison bad luck, even me. I had seen him go many blocks and miles out of the way to keep from having to pass a jail or prison. That's why I was shocked to see him with mom. She thought if he would listen to anyone, it would be me.

The visiting room was large and it had a cigarette, candy and soda machine along with comfortable chairs. He had to stop and talk to practically everyone in the visiting room. Everyone was just as surprised as I was to see him.

As soon as he started in our direction, someone else called him over. Mom began to tell me about him, and I could see and sense that she was really afraid for him. Unbeknownst to me, he had been shot on two separate occasions. But that didn't slow him down any. Now, I had to talk to him. I had to try the impossible: make him see that it was foolish to continuously tempt fate.

"Softy," I called him over, "did you come to see me or everyone else in Lorton?"

He grabbed my hand with a wide grin on his face; I looked into his eyes and it was plain to see he was high from heroin.

"What's up, bro?"

"I'm trying to hold on till things get better, little bro."

"Try not to worry about it. I got an iron in the fire for you."

He sat down beside mom, and I sat in a chair facing them. And I began to talk to him.

"What is going on with you? I've been getting some crazy reports on you, and you know you can't continue robbing those dealers and get away with it. Don't you see that, Softy?"

"Ah Bro! Don't get soft on me."

"Of course, I've changed, yet I'm the same, Softy. Don't you know that? The only thing that has changed about me is my style. The things we did yesterday, we can no longer do them today and survive. Times have changed, Softy, and if we don't change with them, they will destroy us completely. It is the fool that totally disregards the handwriting on the wall."

I looked at my mother and saw all the hurt and pain in her eyes. I gently took her hand in mine. "Look Softy! Look what we have done to the one woman in the world who has always loved us the most. Look at the wrinkles under her eyes. Who do you think put them there? Look," I pointed to one string of gray hair in her head. "Where did it come from? Just look at what we have done to the one woman in the whole world who has always loved us the most." I knew how he loved her, and I was making an emotional plea for his life.

"I guess you're right, bro, but it ain't easy."

"Nothing really is, Softy. Nothing really is."

I knew I had touched him. It was clear we both needed to do something with our lives, but we didn't know what it was or where to go. I talked until I was hoarse. I talked till it was time for them to leave. With all my heart, I hoped my words had not fallen on deaf ears, but deep down inside I had a feeling it had. I knew him, and I knew nothing could or would stop him but death.

"Anything you want or need, bro, send somebody to me, and I'll make sure you get it. But you know better than to look for me down here again, don't you?"

"Yeah," said mom, "it was a miracle I could drag him down here this time. This is the most superstitious boy I've ever seen."

"Take care, bro," I said as he was leaving. I had a gut feeling if he didn't slow down, I would never see him alive again. Had I known what lay just around the corner, I would have held him that day and never let him go.

Two days later a friend that went to the city every day on work release told me he had stopped in Northeast on his way back in, and Softy had just left. He had robbed everybody in the house.

"Cheese, that's the craziest man I have ever seen. He'll hit anyone regardless of the consequences."

Now the clock was ticking for him, and his time was almost up. I wanted to help him, but my hands were tied. All his life he had followed me, and look where I had led him. If I wanted him to be a better person, then why couldn't I?

How could I tell him to do what I wouldn't do myself and expect him to listen? Was I wiser because I was older? Because he never listened, could I interpret that to mean he didn't see? Oh no! He could see, and I wasn't necessarily the wiser. He had to live his life for himself just as I had to live mine. My life was not good enough for him, and his life was too rough for me.

The following week they called me for another visit, and I thought it was mom with the kids. But I got another surprise; it was Jean. This was her first visit to see me since I had been in Lorton.

She was simply beautiful. She brightened the visiting room with a radiant light that seemed to cast a spell on everyone there. Visitors momentarily discontinued their conversations to look in her direction. Convicts looked at her with lust, and I looked at her full with pride and admiration. For some reason, my mind flashed back to the night I first saw her, and I tried to compare her with then and now. But there was no comparison. I had never seen her look more lovely, and I had never seen her glow quite like this. My mind played tricks on me as she strolled towards me. She still had that walk that made men fantasize about their wildest dreams. Every step that she took, my heart vibrated like thunder in my chest. And I never loved her more than I did at that very moment.

After things were settled and back to normal, several inmates, some who knew Jean but had not seen her for a while, began to call us.

"Girl, where have you been hiding?" "Where is my little man?"

"Hey, Cheese, she's still the baddest girl in town."

We responded to their small chatter, and I kissed her affectionately, and we sat down to talk. She sat on the comfortable two-seat sofa, and I sat in a straight-back chair facing her. She sat with her knees between my legs, and her tight dress rose revealing a portion of her lovely thighs. Again, my mind began to play tricks on me. We had a game we played. With all the lust within me, I looked directly into those large beautiful eyes and down at her chocolate thighs. When I looked back into her eyes, we both lit the visiting room up with laughter.

"Cheese, I'm sorry for not getting down here like I should, but you know how much I love you, and…"

"Hush," I stopped her. I shook my head trying to clear it from the lies, games, and deceit. I had rehearsed a speech in my head and went over it a thousand times for this exact moment. I loved her so much, and now it was time for me to show her how much I really loved her. I had to do something that would take years for her to understand. I had to step out of the play just for a moment for the woman I loved.

"Cheese, I love and miss you so much…"

"Hush, baby," I stopped her again. "Let me tell you what's on my mind while I still have the courage." I could have painted her a picture, a beautiful picture, and she would have held on to it like a drowning man would grab and hold a straw. But I couldn't because I loved her too much.

"Jean, I can't sell you a dream. For the first time in my life, I'm in so much trouble that I don't know what to do."

"NO, you've been in trouble before many times, but you always came back."

"Listen to me, baby. Please listen to me. I got a M-1 charge in P.G. County, and if I'm found guilty there isn't but two sentences they can give me, death or life in prison. That's not a dream, baby. That's reality. I'm no longer there with you to hold your hand, wipe your eyes when you cry, protect you from crazy lunatics, and take care of you. Look at me, Jean, I can't even take care of myself."

I saw small tears fall from the corner of her eyes. She had never heard or seen me like this before. Even I was getting all choked up, but I had to continue while I still had the courage.

"How many chumps have hit on you already?" I didn't give her a chance to answer because I was sure there had been many. "Oh yeah, they're going to keep on coming. They are going to try to come in the back door on you with their smooth talking lies and B.S. They're going to promise you the world, but they'll end up giving you nothing but bad times and the blues. Jean, you're going to have to stand all alone in the 20th century as a black woman with two small children, and that will not be so easy. You'll lie awake on cold, lonely nights and call my name, but I will not be able to reach you. And memories will be a poor substitute for the real thing."

"Will you stop talking like that? No matter what happens, I'll be with you always. Don't give up on me now, Cheese." She was no longer crying.

"I guess what I am trying to say is, whatever you do from this point on, I'll understand. Whatever you do, do it with your eyes open, and do it because you want to do it. I don't want you ever feeling guilty that you misled me, betrayed me, or feel unfaithful. In our hearts we will always belong to each other, and you will always be mine."

"But you know can't nobody have me but you, and I don't want nobody but you."

"I hear what you're saying, and I love you for it, but don't be a fool, baby. I'm a dead man, and all I need now is a grave song."

"Stop talking like that. Come what may, I am staying with you." "Well, the final decision is yours, but I've placed all my cards on the table, and I don't want you under false illusions." Now I was choked up again. I knew without a doubt that the dream we had once lived was over; it was dead and gone. But she couldn't see it nor would she believe it. She had witnessed me pull a rabbit out of the hat so many times she really thought I was a magician. It would be years before she understood what I was trying to tell her.

We talked about the children, and how Softy was taking care of them, but I knew he would. She and Softy had always been extremely close. I held her hand and thought about the past, present and future. I thought about the night long ago when we first met, and all the days and nights we had spent together that were too good to utter or write on paper. We talked about P.G. County and when I was scheduled for my next hearing. We talked until the guard announced my name to terminate my visit.

She didn't want to leave, and I really didn't want her to go. We kissed and said good-bye, not realizing what fate had in store for either of us. She walked away smiling, believing that everything would be all right. Several times she looked over her shoulder and blew me a kiss on her way out of the door. I stood there frozen in my tracks with a lump in my throat and a pain in my heart because part of me was going with her. One part of me wanted to scream, "Come back, Jean. I didn't mean a word I said. Please don't leave me alone." But the other part of me said, "Don't be a fool. You can't call back yesterday."

I went back to my dorm thinking about her and the children. I lay awake all night, and in the early morning hours, my soul began to cry, "Yesterday, yesterday, why can't I call back yesterday?"

As my trial date got closer, I waited for an extradition hearing. For some reason, I felt somewhat safe because I knew they could not proceed with a trial until I had a hearing. I waited, but they never called.

I usually watched the news every evening, but this particular night I hung out on the compound with Nae and my friends until 11 p.m. I noticed and sensed that something wasn't quite right when I returned to my dorm, but I couldn11 recognize what it was.

The following morning I had to go to court on an unrelated charge. All I had to do was make an appearance before the court for a matter of record. Jean was there, my mother also, and I thought that was rather unusual. As soon as I sat down between the two marshals on the far side of the courtroom, I read Jean's lips.

"Softy, Softy," was all she said.

I looked at her bewildered, puzzled and confused. Softy! What was she trying to tell me? What was she saying? Everyone had a solemn expression. What is going on? I thought. This was a courtroom, not a funeral. When the judge entered and the court came to order, the attorney immediately made an oral motion.

"Your Honor, I would like to make an oral motion that Mr. Cheese be allowed to visit his brother who is in D.C. General Hospital. He was shot last night and is lying in a coma not expected to live." Softy! Softy shot! What did he mean, what was going on? Softy in a coma?

I sat there, my mind trying to make a connection with what my ears had just heard. I looked out at the same crowd of faces, but I saw nothing. Shot! Shot! My mind was still trying to make a connection. Then it hit me like Muhammad Ali had struck me flush on the chin. They had finally got him. But somehow, like always, he would be all right. I was sure of it. I would make a wager on it. He had to. He simply had to because I couldn't live without him.

Without hesitation, the judge signed the order for me to visit him. The marshals took me to a holding cell where I waited for transportation. I paced the floor with my mind suspended in space trying to figure out how much more the human soul could endure.

It was early afternoon when the two marshals took me to D.C. General Hospital to see him. My mother was there along with some of my relatives. My mother escorted me and the marshals into his room. As strong as I was mentally, I was not prepared for what I saw. I really didn't know how to pray, and I knew nothing about prayer. But I found myself saying, "Lord, please give me the strength. Don't let my mother see me fall apart. I need the strength of someone stronger than I, and I don't know where else to go."

I was in shackles and chains, and I saw him lying there. He had been shot four times, once in both arms, once in the abdomen and once in the head. Tubes were in his nose, mouth and arms. His head was twice its normal size, and his face was swollen so badly that I could hardly recognize him.

Lord! Just let me stand a little while longer. Don't let me break down now. His head was at an angle and it rested on his left shoulder. Both arms were stretched out at his side. Old and fresh tracks (needle marks) ran up and down his arms from his wrists to his underarms. It looked as if someone had taken a knife and sliced his arms to shreds.

Very slowly, as if sleep walking, I moved closer to his bedside. My mother stood at the foot with a handkerchief in her hand covering her mouth.

"Softy, Softy," I said just above a whisper.

"He can't hear you, baby, he can't hear you."

I looked around at her, and she was wiping the tears from her eyes with the handkerchief.

"Softy," I called again. "It's me, little brother. It's me, and everything is going to be all right now." I felt her hand on my arm as she continued to weep. She tried to hold back the tears, but she couldn't. "Just a little while longer, Lord, a little while longer. Give me strength."

After spending time with him, I said good-bye to him, my mother and my relatives. I left in pain and heavy-hearted. I was marched away again in chains, and I rode back to Lorton in silence.

When I got back, I found out my friends had heard the news on television that night I was out roaming the compound. When I asked them why they hadn't told me about Softy, they told me they didn't know how. In olden days, they knew the king killed the messenger who brought bad news. When night fell I had another sleepless night, and my soul cried yesterday, yesterday, why can't we bring back yesterday?

A few weeks later Softy was still in a coma, and I was transported to P.G. County. I thought I was going for a preliminary hearing, but I wasn't sure. I was certain it wasn't for trial because I hadn't had my extradition hearing. The U.S. marshals transported me directly to the P.G. County Courthouse. I was placed in a holding cell with other men from the county jail who had court appearances that day. Suddenly my mental alarm sounded. Something was wrong, and I didn't like the signals I was receiving.

The lawyer came back to the cell and nervously informed me I was going to trial.

"Trial!" I screamed and leaped to my feet. "Have you completely lost your mind? What are you doing to me? I haven't been extradited, and I can't go to trial."

Suddenly I saw that lady justice had put back on its blindfold. The judge had waived my preliminary hearing and deceived me. Here I was expecting a fair fight, and they had taken the fight to the alley. Legally, I thought they were breaking their own law. How could I be tried in Maryland without being extradited from Washington?

Well, if this was the way they were going to play the game, I'll use it as a strategy move. If the jury found me guilty, I was sure to win a new trial on appeal and walk away the victor. No higher court in the land would uphold a conviction of a lower court which had violated a defendant's constitutional rights. Didn't they realize I was still under the jurisdiction of the federal government? I was a federal prisoner serving a federal sentence. Whatever the outcome, I had to go back to Lorton and complete my sentence. Then they would have hell getting me back. I didn't get into the courtroom that day, and the marshals didn't pick me back up. At the end of the day, I was marched across the parking lot to the county jail with the remaining prisoners. They kept me separated from the other prisoners in a tight security cell. All I could do was pace the floor thinking about tomorrow.

Although I was charged with a capital offense, the trial seemed to last only a short minute. And that minute was more than the State of Maryland thought I had coming. It began late one afternoon and was over early the following day. Defendants with petty larceny charges spent more time in court than I had, and the maximum sentence for petty larceny was 18-months!

The State presented what they called an air-tight case. The State had five witnesses to testify against me and three claimed to have been co-defendants. They said that, out of desperation to pull a bankroll together, I had planned the robbery of a drug dealer and committed the murder. But naturally, they lied. They never told the whole truth. And I couldn't present my side to the jury. Because of my criminal record, I couldn't take the witness stand. That would have been absolutely foolish. I would have done more damage than good, so I was forced to listen to their story and remain silent.

It took the jury less than two hours to reach a verdict. When they returned from the jury room, the foreman read the verdict of GUILTY. I stood before the jury and judge not feeling a thing. How could I? It was like I was already dead, and nothing seemed to matter anymore.

It was January, 1974, and the judge set a sentencing date for February. After I was sentenced, still being under the jurisdiction of the federal government, I was supposed to have been transported back to Lorton to complete my sentence with the feds, but once they got me in Maryland they kept me and I never went back to Lorton. According to my understanding of the law, the state of Maryland violated the law because they never gave me an extradition hearing.

In the county jail, they still kept me isolated from the other prisoners. But every night after I showered, I was permitted to make a phone call home. Softy was still in a coma, mom had joined the church and given her life to Christ, and I was waiting to be sentenced for murder. I thought that nothing else could go wrong. I thought there was nothing else the world could do that would affect me, but I was wrong.

I called home one night to discover that the bottom had gone out of the little world I had left. A soon as I heard my sister's voice, I knew something was wrong.

"What's wrong, Daisy?" I asked.

"We don't want you to worry, and there is nothing you can do, but…"

"But what, sis?"

There was a long silence. Then there was a deep sob. "Our brother just died."

My mother picked up the phone in another room, and they were both talking at the same time. I heard sounds, but I couldn't understand what either of them was saying because my mind had gone blank, and I couldn't speak. I cried out with Job, "Why died I not from the womb? Why did I not give up the ghost when I came out of the belly?" How much more could the human mind bear before it shattered into a thousand fragments? How many more steps could I take before I became a permanent member of the insane?

"You are all we have left now. Please — don't do anything foolish. Do you hear me?"

I held the receiver so tight in my fist that my hand ached. Slowly, my mind and voice came back and I was able to speak. "I'm all right. I'm all right." That was all I could say.

I don't recall how I got back to my cell. Time had lost all meaning. I sat on the side of my bunk with tears streaming down my face. I cried until I was physically weak as scenes of our lives flashed before my face. I recalled how we used to argue and fight as kids. I remembered how fast life had passed us by and how quickly we grew into manhood. I remembered when I always went away, he would stand like a vanguard protecting the family like a bear protects its cub. I remembered how angry I was with him when I found out he was shooting heroin. I remembered how he had the instinct for showing up whenever I was in trouble. I remembered how much I really loved him, and I wondered if I could go on without him.

We all die a little death every time we lose someone we love. We ache, we hurt, we grieve and we agonize. All night I cried. And all night my soul cried, yesterday, yesterday, why can't I bring back yesterday? I cried until the morning sun broke the sky with a ray of light into my cell. Morning had come, but the pain had not gone away.

I wasn't permitted to attend his funeral or even view his body. They said I was a security risk, and they weren't taking any chances. They figured I had nothing to lose and everything to gain. I thought about him, Chester, Fly Charles and Cindy. They were all once a part of my life, but now they quietly slept in the bosom of the earth. And I never had the chance to tell them good-bye.

The morning I was going for sentencing one of the deputies in the control center stopped us. "Is that Cheese you have with you?"

"Yes," one of them responded.

"When he comes back from sentencing, let me know. I have to call the marshals to come and pick him up. He has to go back to Washington to complete his sentence."

I stood before Judge William Bowie and listened to his little speech before he pronounced sentence.

"Young man, I see that you have been incarcerated a number of times, and it appears you have not learned from your past incarcerations. You have been found guilty by this court for first degree murder, robbery and the use of a handgun. Do you have anything to say before the court pronounces sentence?"

I wanted to tell him he couldn't kill a dead man, but I stared into his cold eyes and said, "No, I don't, your Honor."

He sentenced me to life and five years in prison. When I went back to the jail, they didn't notify the marshals about me. They immediately put me in a van and rushed me to my new home, the Maryland Penitentiary. My money, clothes and personal items were still in Lorton. I was still a federal prisoner serving a federal sentence, and I had never been released from their custody. I had never been extradited. Yet my destination was the Maryland Penitentiary. And I didn't know what else fate had hidden in the dark for me.

2

Summer of '85

It had been a long, hot, frustrating day. It was one of those extremely hot days that seemed to last forever. The meteorologist had reported that the temperature soared over one hundred degrees at 3 p.m. So it was behind the walls of the Maryland State Penitentiary, the day had finally come to an end. The guards had made their eleven o'clock p.m. rounds and everything was secure for the night.

Although it was almost midnight, I lay straight out across my bunk sweating and wondering how I had survived another day. Suddenly an old familiar thought entered my head: will there be a tomorrow for me? Will I have a heart attack and die before I can summon help? Will an unknown enemy fire bomb my cell and burn me to a crisp? For all I know, this night might be my last. There may not be a tomorrow for me, and I may not see the rising of another morning sun. Apparently, I dozed off to sleep with these thoughts on my mind. The last thing I recalled was the feel of a refreshing breeze that blew into my cell. Everyone was fast asleep. The only sounds that could be heard were those coming from prisoners snoring, gritting their teeth and having occasional nightmares.

Suddenly I heard the voice of a prisoner on a tier above me cry out in the night. It was a strange, unfamiliar and alien sound. It was a pitch that seemed to literally split the night in half. It was a horrible tone, it was so frightening, so terrifying, it shattered one's nerves and smashed one's skull like a wine maker crushed his grapes. Two words he screamed. It was like a wounded animal crying out in the night." OH W-H-Y!" I lay there paralyzed, wondering what kind of soul possessed a man to produce such an insane cry. What experiences could he have lived through? He told his life story, his entire life was lived and told in those two horrifying words, OH WHY! I attempted to put a face with that voice, but his image eluded me. But that sound explosion I will never, ever forget.

"Cheese, did you hear that?" a familiar voice shouted.

I lay there in total silence unable to utter a sound. After all these years I had spent in prison was my mind finally playing tricks on me? Was I hallucinating, hearing sounds that no human voice could produce? Was I imagining it all?

Where did it all begin? How did it all start? The road to prison is only a step away. It could be any number of things. It could be an impulse, pride, a slip of the tongue, a wrong thought, a drink too many or the lust for a woman. However, the road that leads from prison could be one thousand deaths away. How many crimes had I committed? How many hearts had I broken? How many souls and lives were lost traveling this road to prison?

Now as I glance into the mirror I find it difficult to believe so much time has passed, but as I look closer, my reflection tells a different story. Glancing back, I can vividly see and recall all the stops, good and bad, I made along this rugged road to prison. Glancing back, I walk through the pages of my past, and my mind drifts back to Florida.

It was a very mild and humid day in the month of September, in Panama City, Florida. The year was 1944. I imagine the residents of that beautiful city, bursting with wealth, would have called it another typical day. It is not strange that they named it the sunshine state, a peninsula between the Gulf of Mexico and the Atlantic. It was the vacationer's paradise of the good old South. You could see sweet oranges grow on trees, hear tales of crocodiles roaming the many back swamps, see flowers remain in bloom throughout the year, and see black folks, people of color, who were being born, three out of nine, to mostly poor but proud black parents.

Even then, the climate was so beautiful it was the main attraction for vacationers. They came in huge numbers to relax and rest in the sun. It was a nice place to spend a week or two but rarely would any of them stay. It never occurred to me until many years later why they would never stay. So it was on September 30, 1944, a black man-child was born, and he would not stay either.

That is how I always wanted my story to read, but it can't because it is not exactly the truth. You see, I was really born in Ridgespring, South Carolina, and my family didn't move to Florida until several years later. So whenever I was asked or had to fill out forms that asked for my place of birth, I always lied and put Florida instead of South Carolina. Florida was a glamorous state, and the only people who lived in South Carolina were sharecroppers who worked for white folks picking cotton and planting tobacco from "can't see in the morning to can't see at night."

When my parents moved to Florida, they had already established a family that consisted of two boys and one girl. I was the oldest boy, born twenty months after my sister. We were a happy family, and my earliest childhood memories are those of Florida.

My parents were honest and hardworking people. They were firm believers in the great American way, and they dreamed and lived by this very ideal. Had they not seen their people rise from the very bottom to reach the pinnacle in the land of opportunity? But how were they to know that their dreams were artificial dreams in a land that could never be real? How was he to know in the year of '47, when he had so little insight into life, and she was so young, that their America was not in truth like they saw it at all? How were they to know their great America was in reality a capitalistic society, and the strong took unfair advantage of the weak, and the wealthy just plain ignored the poor, and racism was the order of the day, and white folks stayed as far away from the blacks as they could get, and there were no man-made laws then, or now, that said they had to do different?

We were a happy family, and they were deeply in love and devoted to each other. I guess they thought like all other lovers of their day that their love would last a lifetime. But how were they to know that all things change in time? The whole world changes. We change, and so does love. They say the day I was born my father's dream came true, but how was he to know that one day his dream would turn into a curse? I can recall everything going so well, and nowhere in the future was anything suppose to go wrong. Nothing could have been better. Suddenly that dark dragon from ages unknown raised its ugly head to bring about the beginning of our end, and everything began to go wrong. Like a flash of lightning, tragedy invaded our world leading to an unhappy and disastrous ending. There would be no more laughter, there would be no more smiles and happy songs, there would be no more days that we'd wish would never end.

After arriving home one evening, we found our new home burned almost to the ground. All of our possessions, everything of value was destroyed in that fire. It was a terrible loss. We had to move into a small apartment until we could regroup, but the loss had left my parents empty and depressed. We began to see for the first time our mother and father drift apart. Then that ugly dragon raised its gruesome head again.

My father had a stroke that left him partially paralyzed on his left side. He could no longer practice his trade (stone mason), and for the first time in his life, he became a member of the unemployed. My parents began to have terrible fights.

His pride was gone, and the light which once shined so bright from his eyes became duller and duller until one day it finally went completely out. He became withdrawn and was never home. I guess it became too much for his once proud soul, because one day he disappeared, and I don't even remember him saying goodbye.

Call it a tragedy or fate, but life for my family would never be quite the same. I guess it is typical for a father to want his son to be in many ways like himself. But he would never live to see all the dreams he had for me come true. We lived in two different worlds, a generation apart. He would never know anything about my world, nor would I ever know anything about the world in which he lived, slaved, and died.

He left before I really had the chance to know him. I would often hear other little kids brag and boast about the mighty deeds of their fathers, and I would begin to hate him for deserting me so early in life. But I think if he could have somehow gazed into a crystal ball on the night of my birth, he never would have allowed the doctor to start the beat of my heart.

So much time has passed since then, and it seems like I've died over a thousand deaths since that night so long ago. Every time I was arrested for a crime I was accused of committing, everything seemed different when I was locked in a cold cell all alone. It was those times I became frightened and I wasn't so tough after all. Here I would see my situation crystal clear. I'd see the death, brutality, and violence in every wicked and heartless manner, and I would tremble with fear. In prison, your life was valueless and had no more worth than the effort it took to produce it, and I would cry out for help. You see, when you are alone, there is no one to impress, no one to tell you how brave you are, no one to pat you on the back and shake your hand for really being a dam fool. When you are alone, there are no rewards for playing a game, and all you feel is a pain.

When I was about twenty, I heard that my father had been dead for a few years. Now, as I reflect back, I wish things would have been different for us, but life would teach me many valuable lessons. You can't stop time and start over again. Nor can you take back the blow that has already been struck and make the wrong seem right.

Many times I thought about what my life would have been like if my father had stayed with us. My life might have been different. Maybe he could have taught me about his world, and I would have been just like him, but that was just a thought. That was just my weakness speaking out because in my heart I know my life would have turned out precisely as it did.

Every day and every minute the hour hand is moving around the clock, and when one day ends and a new day begins, the wrongs committed in our lives yesterday, can never be put right tomorrow. When I grew up, I always wanted to tell my father, "Dad, now I really understand." But I never did. I wanted him to know that no matter what, he still was my father and in my own confused way, I really loved him—but I just didn't know how to tell him. One day I also would have a son, and he would be named after me just as I had been named after him. Almost twenty years later I would make him a promise that I would never leave or be taken away from him. But that too was a promise I'd never be able to keep. Whereas my father and I lived in two different worlds, the world of my son and me would be exactly the same.

Life would have to teach me there is a price you have to pay for everything you get in life, and the price you have to pay is always more than it is worth. I would be a slow learner, but like my mother said, "A hard head will make a soft behind."

3

Picking Up The Pieces

AFTER THE FIRE AND separation, my mother was left with the task of picking up the pieces. She took what she could salvage, and we went to live temporarily with our grandparents in Ridgespring, South Carolina. To us, it was like going back home, because it was the place of our birth. I had no memories of the South when we had left for Florida, and now it was like seeing it for the first time.

My grandparents lived on a large farm. It was only a short distance from the train station and town itself. In order to reach the farm, there was a long, winding dirt road that twisted and turned for what seemed like miles along an empty road. To reach the house you had to pass by an old wooden structure that had long seen its best days as a barn. The boards were badly beaten from the elements of nature, and now this old worn out barn was only used to store old farm machinery. Now far from the barn, a final curve came to an end in front of a large house.

My grandparents grew a variety of food. There were tomatoes, onions, beans, sweet potatoes, watermelons, peanuts, cabbage, and squash. They owned cows, chickens, a mule, and a few pigs, but their main cash crop was cotton.

This was the first time I could ever remember seeing cotton, and I never imagined so much of it existed in the world. There were gigantic fields of fluffy white balls bursting from the tip of green stalks. There were some rows that seemed to be a mile long, and there was only space for one person to enter a row at a time. The cotton that you picked from stalks went into a burlap sack you carried on your shoulder. When the bags were full, you had to walk to the end of the row and empty them on a large, coarse fabric that lay at the end of these long rows. Some days it was so hot you could see heat waves slowly rising from the ground into the atmosphere.

To protect one's head from the sun, everyone wore large straw hats. At the end of the day the cotton was put on a wagon and taken to the barn to be weighed and later sold by the pound. My grandparents had fifteen children and many grandchildren. Kids then were considered a blessing. The more children you had, the more work you could produce in the fields. On most occasions my grandfather would not come in at noon for lunch. The youngest children would take him his lunch along with ice cold water in a large mason jar.

My grandfather was the hardest working man I had ever seen. He was always in motion. He taught the boys how to hoe a garden, plow a field, fish, and hunt. Often I would hear him repeat, "Young'un, hard work ain't never killed nobody." No, grandpa, hard work didn't kill you, but it did give you a bent back and calloused hands. But all in all, I never once heard him complain.

I can remember thinking when I first saw all this land and crops, "No one couldn't tell me my grandparents were not rich." Little did I know they were just sharecroppers, just like most other Southerners of their generation. They owned nothing, and if they did, it was very little. White people owned the property and the land, and if you weren't careful they could end up owning you.

To me, sharecropping was just another form of modern slavery. One-hundred and twenty-nine years ago President Abraham Lincoln had issued the Emancipation Proclamation freeing the Negroes and abolishing slavery. But for the Negroes, what did that really mean? So what did freedom for Negroes mean? Did it mean we would be treated as equal to whites? Did it mean we would finally be treated as first class citizens and enjoy the opportunities that America offered its other citizens? True, we were freed on paper, but in practice we were still treated as slaves, and sharecropping was just another form of slavery that helped maintain the economy of the South.

America had made us good slaves. The less it gave us, the more we were made to feel appreciative. The psychological effects as well as the impact of slavery was disastrous for us as a nation of people. But the process of making a good slave was not a swift nor an easy task.

First, the slave master had to maintain strict discipline among the slaves. He cultivated the Negroes so that they would always think and feel subordinate. Then they implanted in the slaves' consciousness a sense of inferiority, and they were made to know their place and feel the large gap that existed between master and slave. They were made to feel this was their natural state—the way it should be and would always remain. Slaves were also made aware of their master's powers. Many slaves were forced into believing that it was the masters who held the power of life and death in their hands over them. They were forced to take an active part in the wellbeing of the master, and whatever the master did to them, no matter how horrible, it was done for their benefit. They were made to feel helpless and totally dependent on the slave master for their entire existence.

Now, some ingenious mind had developed the system of sharecropping, and eighty-four years after Mr. Lincoln's Emancipation Proclamation, the system of sharecropping still maintained the institution of slavery. Here the slave master had changed his name to overseer, and my grandparents worked the land for a very small percentage of the profit. Oh yeah, we were free on paper, and on many legal documents it was written, "All men are by nature free and equal," but on the outside in the burning sun, under the whip of the overseer, the Negro slaves cried out in pain.

Later in life I would recognize other modern American slave systems that were built on the principles of slavery. I would spend half a lifetime attempting to break a vicious cycle of one of these systems of which I had freely become a modern day slave. Later, prisons would replace sharecropping and blacks would be used to produce the labor. Many would disagree and say our Race as a whole has made tremendous progress and has come a long way. But to them I'll say, if we have come a long way, it is only because what we have been chasing has run twice as far. The more things change the more they stay the same.

My grandparents were the most generous people I have ever known. I never heard them say an unkind word about anyone. When I say sharecropping is a curse, they say it was a blessing. They were wise and full of wisdom. They were firm but gentle and loved all of their grandchildren dearly. Their outstanding characteristic was rooted in their strong faith and belief in God.

There was only one school and church for blacks in town. We went to school five days a week and church on Sunday. I can still see that old-fashioned pot-belly stove in the corner. One teacher taught all the required subjects, and teachers ruled with an iron hand and their word in the classroom was the law. Truancy was unheard of, and the teachers were not afraid to discipline you with whatever punishment was necessary, including the use of a strap. School was considered a privilege and education was strongly emphasized.

Parents made great sacrifices for their children; they understood then that education was a key, and they wanted their children's future to be better than their rigid past. Since there were no hot school lunches for us in those days, we took biscuits and a piece of greasy pork in a brown paper bag; this was the only lunch we knew. Still, my generation had it much better than my parents. My mother had to walk two and one half miles to school, and two of those miles she said were in the woods. She had to drop-out of school in the fifth grade to go to work in the field. I guess I was truly blessed to be born in a generation where parents put their children before themselves. So they pushed and motivated us and dreamed that we would rise higher and go farther than their previous generation of sharecroppers.

After we had been with our grandparents for a short while, my mother received a letter from one of her sisters who was living in Greensboro, North Carolina; she told her of the many opportunities and how easy it was to advance. She had a job as a clerk in a local dry cleaners.

This was the generation where black people moved North in a search of the Promised Land. They migrated North leaving the South behind to work in the factories and plants of the Northern cities. They had grown tired of picking cotton, milking cows, and working in tobacco fields. They were trying to make a better life for themselves and their children, and my mother was no exception.

My mother left us in the care of our grandparents and off she went to the Promised Land. She would send for us as soon as she acquired a job and a place for us to live. This was the first time we were separated from our mother. Although we were with our grandparents, we missed her very much.

It didn't take my mother long to secure employment and a small apartment. She sent our grandparents the train fare, and they took us to the train station. We boarded the train in tears. We would miss our wonderful grandparents, but we were going to be with our mother. We didn11 know it then but every year afterwards, we would ride these same rails back and spend every summer with our grandparents. This would give us a short vacation and my mother a chance to catch her breath.

The conductor on the train was a little old black man with a head full of gray hair. Our grandparents told him our destination and that we would be traveling alone. He was very kind and friendly to us, and he watched us very closely. He made sure we were as comfortable as possible, and I'm sure he wanted to make certain we arrived at our destination safely.

This was our first train ride, but it would not be our last. We kept our faces pressed to the window enjoying the beautiful scenery. The ride seemed to last forever. The sun had set and darkness was slowly creeping over the face of the earth, covering the world with its blackness, but still the train rolled on into the night.

"Greensboro, Greensboro, next stop Greensboro, North Carolina," the conductor shouted. My sister and I had to wake our little brother who was fast asleep. The conductor approached us with a smile on his face, "Get ready kids." Then he began to get our bags and luggage from the compartment overhead. "This is your stop coming up."

Nervously, we made preparation to leave the train. We were jittery and full of anticipation.

"Make sure you have all of your belongings," the little old man said. He stood there with our bags in both hands. We would have been lost without his aid. Finally he led us off the train to meet our mother. This was to be our home for over the next decade. This was a thrilling and heart-stirring moment for us, the day we had waited and longed for had finally arrived.

Our mother was there to sweep us off our feet with a happy smile across her face: she appeared fresh, vigorous, and so full of life. She had a thousand questions to ask. "How is your grandparents? How was the trip?" We were so happy and so overwhelmed, we all tried to answer her at the same time.

This was our mother, and we were all together again. We were united. We were one big happy family. She didn't have a husband, and we no longer had a father with us, but we had each other and that was important. She had her children, and we had our mother, so what could possibly go wrong. Little did we realize that old dragon would always be just a step away, snapping at our heels like a hound-dog chasing prey.

Greensboro would not be like South Carolina and Florida. Now we had no father; there was no new house or automobile, no property, money stashed away or security. All we had now was each other. Our mother would have to raise her children alone the best she knew how. She was young and she would have to stand alone in America in the '50s with three children, but the world would not be so kind to her. It would be brutal, cruel, rough, and tough for a black woman who attempted to stand alone. Little did I know, that years later my brother and I would cause her the greatest pain of all. The hurt that we caused her would be like an invisible hand that seemed to reach inside her bosom to snatch out her heart and to trample upon it in the North Carolina mud. On one hand we gave her love, but on the other hand, we gave her too much hurt and pain.

Greensboro was the second largest city in the state. It was the home of A&T State University and Bennett College. It was a calm and beautiful place, and the people were easy to live with. They were friendly, peaceful, polite, generous, proud, and decent. They worked five days a week, gave parties on the weekends, and went to church on Sundays. If you were less fortunate, they would share without hesitation, and if you were in need they would come to your aid.

These were the people of Greensboro when we first arrived. But soon times would change; the world would change, and so would these proud and kind people.

The most common laws that were violated were gambling and bootlegging whiskey. Seldom would their activities extend beyond these. Of course you had the usual barroom fight where someone would get injured with a knife or Saturday night special. And there was always the domestic disturbance where the husband had one too many drinks and later take his frustration out on his family. But usually the community took care of its own.

I spent the days of my youth growing up in this town that I slowly came to love. I was the oldest boy, so naturally I had to be the man of the house. My sister and I often fought for this title. She thought since she was the oldest child she should be the head in my mother's absence, but our fights would usually end in a tie.

We were a private and close-knit family that stood against the odds. Our apartment was small, clean and comfortable. It was located on Coaston Street not far from the city boundary. It was a long, rocky dirt road with woods on one side and a few scattered houses on the other.

This was in the early '50s, and we enrolled in Washington Street Elementary. Our first school experience had been in Ridgespring, so we had very little trouble readjusting to school and making friends. But on several occasions we heard snickering and giggling behind our backs because we didn't quite talk and dress like the other students.

To be certain we had all the necessary requirements for school, Mother worked two jobs, sixteen hours every day. She came home at 6:30 in the morning, got us prepared for school, and when we left, she went out with us to catch the bus to work on her second job. All she did then was work and make sure we had the things we needed. How many times did I see her deny herself for the sake of her children? For instance, if there was only enough food for three, suddenly she was not hungry. She always stood in between us and the rest of the world, not because she loved us so little, but because she loved us so very much.

From Coaston Street we moved into a small house on Willow Road. After this we seemed to move from one place to another. We were like traveling gypsies, and it seemed like my mother was still in search of the Promised Land. She had to work harder now than she did in the cotton fields in the South. But I guess it always looked greener on the other side.

By this time my mother had entered into a relationship for the first time since my father left. Soon we had a stepfather, and from their union she gave birth to her last child; we had another brother and now there were four of us. My relationship with my stepfather was a love/hate one. I loved hi m, but most of the time I hated him. Although I didn't really know my father, still I didn't think my stepfather was good enough to take his place.

The years passed swiftly. At thirteen I began to hook school and cut classes. When I did go, I went because of the girls. I would put a mirror on my shoe to look underneath their clothes. Other times I'd pull my chair close behind theirs and put my knee on their butts. When I was in the eighth grade

I completely lost all interest in school. I sat in the class room and daydreamed, and never took books home or did my homework.

Deep inside I had a feeling that something was out of place. I had gotten tired of learning about white folk's history and nothing about my own. Somehow I felt like an observer and that nothing being taught was related to me, and when it was, it was always with a negative view: little black Sambo, Dick and Jane, Columbus discovered America, and Lincoln freed the slaves because he was a great lover of humanity. Lies—all lies; and if we were not being taught the truth in school, where could we go for the truth?

How was little black Sambo and Dick and Jane related to me? If Columbus really discovered America, then that means no one was here on this continent when he arrived. And the biggest lies of all, Lincoln freed the slaves because he was a great humanitarian. In the last paragraph of the Proclamation Lincoln himself said, "It was sincerely believed to be an act of justice, warranted by the Constitution upon military necessity." Yet, the system perpetuated a lie and penalized me for not believing.

I guess I grew up much too fast; I never really had or took the time to be a child. I was always trying to act out the roll of being a man. My mother would often call me her little man, and I felt this was the highest compliment she could give. Being that she worked, because my father was never at home, the least I could do was take care of the house and look after my sister and brothers, but I didn't.

I began to stay out late at night and drink cheap wine. I had a best friend named Doug, and we did all the mischievous things that most youngsters did at that time. We committed petty and minor thievery, but we had most of our fun at the dances. We got intoxicated and went to dances at the local YMCA and recreation centers. We danced to the latest records, and sometimes local bands provided the music. We were both good dancers, and all the girls enjoyed dancing with us. We hung out together until I went away, but when I returned things were never the same with us.

But in the mean time I was still trying to be a man. I was doing things the way I thought a man would do them. But my idea of a man was distorted by these characters I had seen playing out their rolls as if they were actors in a play. But I didn't know that this was not a play. This was the real thing, but I was beginning to live it as if it was a practice run. Little did I know that life could be so short and the dreams we dream so very far away. Had I known this, maybe I would have danced to the beat of a different drummer. But how was a dumb kid like me to know that all our deeds, good or bad or right or wrong, are recorded on the pages of the book of our life?

Soon I was fifteen and stood six feet tall, and I thought I was a man. I began to hang out in pool-rooms and drink wine every day. Most nights I stayed out very late or didn't go home at all. My stepfather no longer was at home. My sister kept the house while my mother worked and my brother and I ran the streets. He was fifteen months younger, but he was as brave as any kid I had ever known and had the heart of a lion. We were developing a pattern of life that would call for a violent and early end.

4

Going Astray

IN THE '50S, THE social institutions were a central part of the black social structure. Our society was primarily built on three pillars: the family, the church, and the schools. These pillars served to stabilize our society.

First, the black family was much more than a group of individuals living under the same roof; everyone worked together as a unit for the good of the family. Love was expressed and communicated in many verbal and nonverbal ways. The family was considered as a unit and not a multitude with contrasting concepts and beliefs. The family traveled on the same road moving toward the same destination. There was unity and direction as well as a sense of purpose. Now and then if a child misbehaved in the absence of the parents, most neighbors in that neighborhood had the parents' permission to correct and discipline that child. So in essence, our neighborhood was an extended part of our family.

The church and religion were also strong pillars in our social structure. The pastor's obligation extended far beyond just preaching from the pulpit on Sundays. Maybe he didn't possess a doctorate degree of theology from a prestigious university, but he took an active role in the communities as well as in the activities of our society. In those days, he was considered much more than a pastor. Along with his title went a host of other duties such as psychologist, legal advisor, and doctor. It was not uncommon for a pastor to visit the home and communities, and it was standard for him to visit the hospitals and prisons and pray for the sick.

Equally important were the schools. Most students went to school to learn, and education was then considered a serious business. Parents sacrificed and children were expected to perform. Teachers were dedicated to their profession and took a personal interest in the welfare of the students. Drugs, violence, and teen pregnancy were almost nonexistent in schools in those days. For a student to have a fistfight after school was a major event and talked about for days.

Although I disagreed with the curriculum being taught in the black schools, nevertheless, they strongly reinforced the values and morals instilled in the children at an early age. Consequently, these three pillars, working in conjunction, served to stabilize our society.

Telephones and televisions were not yet that common in the black community; only a few families were able to afford them in the '50s. As a result, the families were closer together. They communicated more. They ate family meals together. They discussed problems and sought resolutions and grew stronger. Years later—much later—the black family and these pillars that had held us together for centuries would collapse and almost deteriorate.

In spite of all my street activities, I still spent quite a bit of time at home and at the local YMCA. I was a member of the swimming team, and my brother was a drill sergeant and played shortstop for the hardball team. Our coach and instructor was Art Stadium; he was a fatherly figure to all of us and a wonder man. He was aware of the close relationship that existed between my brother and me. He was also aware of our street activities, and for this reason he gave us a great deal of attention. He tried his best, I am sure, to pull us away from the streets, but he was fighting a losing battle. The "Y" was an important part of the community and to the youths, and Mr.

Stadium was well-respected by everyone's parents. He encouraged the youths to spend their leisure time at the "Y" and off the streets.

"There is nothing in the streets but trouble and that is spelled with a capital 'T'," he would tell us over and over again.

I guess he realized that once the street got its hooks into us there would be nothing left but instant death and prison cells. He succeeded with some of us, but others of us he just couldn't reach. Unfortunately, I was one of the latter, but I will always love him for trying to show us a better way.

As stable as our social institutions were in the '50s, they still were not able to keep me off the street. I was going through a stage of development where I rebelled against everything that displayed the least sign of authority. Little did I realize it at the time, I was establishing a deviant behavior that would take many long years to break. I was too busy trying to be a man, but I didn't know that life could call a child to manhood so quick and so fast.

This was an era when street gangs were common, and I was a member of one of the gangs for a short period. We had fights against rival gangs. We stole from local stores, hung around the junior high school and tried to extort money from the students. We committed petty crimes, not so much for the money, but for the excitement and challenge. We were seeing how far we could go before someone put a halt to our abnormal behavior.

Greensboro was also celebrated for its achievements in the struggle for civil rights. In the '50s, Greensboro was still very much a segregated town, but in the latter part of the decade, students from A&T State University made history. Dr. King's movement was sweeping the South and it was as if these students could no longer remain silent. They placed their lives on the line fighting for liberties that should have been ours by birth. They fought against discrimination, racism, and the inequities of the South. They staged sit-ins and boycotts, and their cry for freedom was heard around the world.

Discrimination is not new; it is as old as time and the nations themselves. When one race believes by nature it's superior to others, the result is discrimination. No other nation of people has had to suffer slavery in America but African-Americans. We did not come as Pilgrims. We came in chains packed in the in the belly of slave ships with little food and water and without proper sanitation. The European settlers who came to America to avoid punishment and discrimination were themselves the greatest beneficiaries and advocates of the American institution of slavery. Slavery had been an American institution for over a century and a half before the War of Independence.

Parents themselves have always played a role in shaping discrimination. Children are not born with hatreds for people simply because they belong to other social groups. On the contrary, they acquire this hatred from their mothers and fathers through a basic learning process. Now, they overtly discriminate because they think by nature they are superior to blacks and minorities. But we, the descendants of slaves, were placed at a greater disadvantage and became the worst victims of racism and discrimination in all its vicious forms, especially in the South.

The students formed long lines and demonstrated in front of the Woolworth Department Store and other establishments that continued to remain racially segregated. All of their policies were strictly discriminatory. The color of your skin dictated the way you were treated. You could spend your money and purchase food at the lunch counter, but you could not take a seat at the counter and eat with the white customers. Theaters were also segregated; blacks could attend but they had to sit in the balconies. The students were well organized and received local and national support. Week after week participants walked the picket lines and boycotted. Although violence often erupted and many arrests were made, the struggle went on.

There were some who tried to tell these intelligent black students, "Slowdown! Take it easy! Don't rush things. We're going to give you equality in the sweet by and by. After all, didn't this great nation go to war to free the slaves and abolish slavery?"

But the Civil War they were talking about was a myth, because the Civil War was not fought to free the slaves. First, some said it was because of the economy. Others said it was a military necessity. A few had the opinion that it was a humanitarian issue, while others said it was political (states rights vs. federal government). But most held the myth that this war was indeed fought to free the slaves.

First, the South depended upon the slave labor force for its economy. To free the slaves, it would destroy their economic system. As for the military, again, in the last paragraph of the Proclamation, the President stated: "It was sincerely believed to be an act of justice, warranted by the Constitution upon military necessity." So as far as the President was concerned, it was strictly a military necessity.

Then the abolitionists said their cause was humanitarian; they wanted to eradicate the social ills of America. It was morally wrong for one man to own another. But, the single most important issue was the states' rights vs. the federal government. This was the issue that occurred and re-occurred throughout American history. The states claimed to have certain rights. The government agreed, but said the states' rights did not supersede those of the federal government. The states further claimed under the Constitution that the federal government had no power to abolish slavery in those states where it existed. But after the Civil War, this issue was settled once and for all. All states were bound forever to recognize the superior sovereignty of the federal government. So, contrary to popular belief, slavery was the least issue concerning the Civil War, thus making the war they spoke of a MYTH.

It is hard to wait for tomorrow to get what everyone else has today. So, the students continued to protest, march, and demonstrate against discrimination. Finally, their demands were met and integration achieved. This was the dawn of a new day in the South. Those courageous and fearless students brought integration to a town that tried its best to remain in the dark age.

In 1959 was fifteen, and I met a new friend and had my first encounter with the law. My friend's name was Jimmy, and we began to steal cars and go for joy rides. If the keys were not in the cars, he would very quickly hot wire them. As much as he tried to teach me about mechanics, my mechanical knowledge didn't extend beyond driving, but anything you wanted to know about an automobile, Jimmy knew it.

At first we were just having fun, but soon our little fun got serious. Jimmy had the idea it was time to graduate from joy riding to making money.

"We could steal cars and take them across the state line and sell them for cash," he said.

I never thought about making money from stealing and selling cars. I was just having fun, but reluctantly, I agreed. And our first adventure was a disaster. It was late one summer evening. It was dusk dark and rain slowly fell to the ground. We walked the half-deserted streets looking for a suitable car to steal. Jimmy had said that a '58 Chevy would be perfect and easy to sell. We must have walked for hours looking for a '58 Chevy. We went from the business district to the residential district and still no '58 Chevy. I was about to give up because I was tired of walking and my feet were hurting.

"Let's try again tomorrow," I told Jimmy.

We were far out into the white residential neighborhood, and we were headed back toward home. As fate would have it, half of the distance from home, there sat, parked on the street, a red and white '58 Chevy.

"Look!" he said with excitement.

We approached the Chevy with caution. We looked in the passenger's side and saw the keys had been left in the ignition.

"They must have known we were coming," I tried to say with amusement. We quickly got in with Jimmy taking the wheel, and we were on our way. We drove to the nearest gas station and filled the tank with gas.

"Where to now," I looked at him and asked?

"Florida," he replied. I didn't know whether he was serious or not, but I knew it was time for me to get serious. I angrily told him to pull the car over and let me out. There was one thing that I really liked about him; he was a much better talker than I was.

"Cheese, I think it would be a good idea for us to get away from Greensboro for a while. I've always wanted to go to Florida, and we can sell the car down there and have fun for weeks before we come back."

The more he talked the better the idea sounded, and I hadn't seen Florida since we left when I was a child. The better he painted the picture, the better it looked to me until I couldn't wait to hit the highway. That was always one of my weaknesses as a youth; I was easily persuaded and little did I realize it at the time, it would prove to be a mistake. As a youth, you try to tell yourself it really is your choice and you are doing what you want; but you're lying to yourself.

We rode for a long time, and I was trying to tell him what little I remembered about Florida. Soon, we were at the state line. We were leaving the state of North Carolina, and still we rode on into the night. Only a few cars were on the highway, so we had the road to ourselves. We stopped only for food and gas. Somewhere deep in South Carolina, I took the wheel. Jimmy was tired and crawled in the back seat to take a nap.

I didn't mention it, but I had a gut feeling this would be a trip I would never forget. Shortly, I was to find out that feeling was right. I drove until early morning. The sun was slowly creeping across the morning sky when Jimmy crawled back into the front seat.

"Pull over at the next stop," he said trying to wipe the sleep from his eyes. "We can get something to eat and I'll take the wheel."

Our present location was somewhere in Georgia, and that gut feeling began to nag me again. To the left of the highway a sign read, Gas & Food. I pulled into the entrance and stopped at the nearest gas pump.

"Fill it up with regular," Jimmy called from the passenger side.

I opened the door and got out. "You can have the wheel now," I told him. I noticed on the corner of this old white washed building a faded sign that said, Restroom. It didn't say, White ONLY: it just said, Restroom.

"I'm going to take a leak," I said. And then I headed toward the sign that said, Restroom. As I turned the corner, there were two doors on each of the buildings; one said, Men and the other said,

Women. Again, it didn't say White ONLY. It just said. Men & Women. I went in the door that said, Men.

I was urinating in the toilet when suddenly the door burst open.

"What are you doing in here n-i-g-g-e-r?" a hate-filled voice screamed from the open door.

I didn't bother to turn around because I was sure it was Jimmy playing one of his practical jokes.

But again, the bitter voice screamed louder and with more rage, "Nigger! Who told you to come in here?"

There stood in the door one of the largest white men I had ever seen; he was as tall as the door and just as wide. Was this that gut feeling manifesting itself? He stood there with his hands at his side balled into a huge fist, his mouth dripping with poisonous venom, and his eyes full of insane prejudice and hatred. "What was I to do?" I thought. Then, the reality of the situation hit me like a ton of bricks.

My mind seemed to speak out loud, "Idiot! You are deep in the state of Georgia, swelling with animosity and hostility towards blacks, and you're taking a leak in a white man's toilet." It didn't have to say, White ONLY. Negroes born in the South knew they were not good enough to use a white man's toilet!

Well, you made a mistake. The only thing he can do is tell you to leave. But, inside I knew it was deeper than that, and it was.

He lunged toward me striking me on the head with one of his huge fists. And at that point, I began to struggle and fight for dear life. I fought with everything I had. I knew if I lost this battle I would also lose my life. I charged at him with both feet and fists, then I would quickly retreat. The small size of the restroom had me at another disadvantage. But as soon as I would retreat, I'd charge again. However, my small hands and feet seemed useless.

When I was in trouble, the first two words that fell from my lips were mother and God. I knew my mother couldn't help me now, so I called on God. "Lord, please don't let me die in Georgia at the hands of this madman."

He was huffing and puffing for air, and I was tired and bleeding from the nose and mouth. Out of desperation I made a final charge. I took aim at his groin and kneed him as hard as I could.

"Ouch! You black…s.o.b," the giant moaned in pain as he fell to the small bathroom floor.

He was lying there with his mouth open in wonder, and for the first time I noticed a small penknife in his right hand. I was really shaking with fear now, but as I stepped across him, I kicked him and I ran out the door.

Jimmy was behind the wheel totally unaware of my skirmish. "It took you long enough to take a leak," he said. "Where were you?"

I was out of breath, but I tried to tell him as quick as possible what had just taken place in the bathroom between the big giant and me. He pulled away from the station so fast the rubber on the tires were burning. Nervously he asked, "Have you completely lost your mind?"

We raced down the two-lane highway, knowing we would hear a police siren at any moment. For miles we traveled but still no siren.

"Everything is cool," I said, "if it wasn't, we would have known something by now."

One hour later on the same highway a state trooper car came from nowhere. The car followed us for another mile.

"Don't panic now," I said. That gut feeling came upon me again, and somehow I had the feeling this was the beginning of the end for Jimmy and me.

Jimmy looked over at me and asked, "Can we outrun them?" "Don't be a fool," I said more out of fear. I was sure if we tried to outrun them or do anything foolish they would kill us, and it didn't matter that we were only fifteen. "Pull over Jimmy."

One trooper approached the car while the other stood back; both of them had their hands on their guns.

The trooper asked, "May I see your driver's license and registration, boys?"

Jimmy sat there looking dumbfounded. He could not produce either a license or registration. I couldn't believe it; this auto genius didn't even have a driver's license. Now, the other trooper was at the car, and they both had their guns drawn and ordered us both out of the car.

"I called in and they reported this car stolen in Greensboro, North Carolina," the other trooper said.

They searched us, handcuffed us, and took us to a small county jail. We were processed, booked, and charged with interstate transportation of a stolen automobile. The crime we had committed was a federal offense, and we would now have to be tried by the feds. Finally, we were placed in different cells awaiting trial.

For the first time in my life I felt all alone. I thought about my family. Did they know where I was? As I thought about them, I knew they would be worried about me and my eyes began to get misty. I called my mother's name over and over again, but she couldn't help me now. I'm so sorry, mom, but she could not hear me either. Jimmy was in a cell two cells down from mine, and we talked all night and slept all day, but I was still lonely. There was a rather attractive female who brought us our meals at lunch and dinner, and we often talked. She wanted to know all about the city. But still I was lonely and wanted to go home. I promised myself to never get involved with crime if I got out of this mess.

At the time I didn't realize I was just a youth going through a state of development. Nothing really seemed to be important. We just lived for the moment. Nothing else really mattered. I was able to masquerade my weakness, as strength. When I was with my young peers, I was able to conceal my true emotions. I permitted their behaviors to dictate my actions. If they were foolish, I was foolish. If they were rowdy, so was 1.1 wanted so desperately to be a part of the in-group, I was willing to pay any price. But, when I was alone, as I am now, I hated myself because I was too weak to be what I wanted to be. I was too weak to say, "NO," this is not what I wanted to be. And, I wondered what the boys would say if they saw these tears falling from my eyes.

We had a preliminary hearing in the federal courthouse, and the judge set a date for our trial, then we were taken back to the county jail. Our future was now in the hands of the judge.

5

Another Chance

"Black men, whether in North or South, have always been skeptical of the courts capacity to administer fair, equal, and impartial justice."

George Jackson

FOR MANY NIGHTS I was unable to sleep in the county jail; there was a constant flow of ideas racing through my mind. On one hand, I day-dreamed, talked to imaginary figures, and had wild fantasies. But on the other hand, I had deep reflections. Here I was only fifteen years old, hundreds of miles from home, with an inevitable date with a federal judge, and I wasn't sure what the outcome would be. What kind of judge would he be? Was it possible he would consider giving me another chance, or would he be severe in his punishment? One thing was certain, time would tell it all.

My thoughts were interrupted by Jimmy hollering from down the block, "How much time do you think the judge will give us, Cheese?"

"I wish I knew; we're strangers in a strange land," I told him. That must have been the tenth time he had asked that in less than twenty-four hours. Deep down inside we were both afraid and frightened, but we were pretending to be tough.

All the time I was corresponding with my mother, she wrote to me regularly and sent money for me to purchase the necessary items I needed. She told me how much the family missed me and everything was going to be all right. She tried desperately to get me to change my lifestyle while I was still a youth and had a chance.

"Now is the time," she wrote, "if you let this opportunity pass, you may never get another." I didn't see how she could be so optimistic. How could she be so sure? What did she know that I didn't? She, of course, didn't know that the system of justice operated like a whorehouse selling itself to the highest bidder. Its primary concern was not guilt or innocence, but who was able to put the highest fee on top of the table.

As our court date got nearer, Jimmy and I talked about our case.

"How are you pleading, Cheese?"

"Like a man with good sense, Jimmy, guilty." We were caught with a red-hot smoking gun, so how else could a man with good sense plea? Besides, I had no illusion about the system of justice. Playing the tough guy role had its time and place but this sure wasn't one of them. We were black, poor and uneducated; and even if we were without sin, we were still guilty. We were born with the guilt of being black! I told him I was pleading guilty mostly because I was too afraid to fight. I told him not to be a fool and do anything else. I wanted to be sure he heard and understood what I was trying to say.

On the day of trial, the federal marshals came and picked us up early in the morning. They put a chain around our waists, opened the handcuffs and put them through a link in the chain and handcuffed us to the chain. We could only move our hands so many inches in either direction. They also put leg-irons on our ankles. I will never forget the look in the people's eyes as we were marched into the courthouse. We were like captured animals on our way to be slaughtered.

Unlike the troopers and local police, the marshals were polite, kind, and professional. They placed us in a small holding cell where we waited our turn to go before the magistrate. They removed the chains, cuffs, and leg-irons and we began to walk and pace the floor. We paced the floor in complete silence, smoking cigarette after cigarette.

"Well Jimmy, I guess this is it," I told him.

He responded in a tone of sarcasm, "From the sound of your voice and the look on your face all we need now is a grave song."

This would be my first experience with the criminal court proceedings. Until this point, my knowledge of the system was mostly hearsay and observation at a distance, but now I would learn from firsthand experience. Preceding our trial, we had been assigned court appointed attorneys, and they visited us on several occasions. They agreed under the circumstances a plea of guilty would be in our best interest.

Under the assigned counsel system, private practicing lawyers were appointed by the court to represent defendants who could not afford to hire an attorney. The Sixth Amendment guaranteed the right of counsel. But that lost most of its meaning when the state determined who that lawyer will be. If the state was allowed to pick lawyers for both sides, the result could often be predicted. Perhaps that is the reason they thought it best for us to plead guilty, or maybe it was the color of our skin and the holes in our pockets.

The judge's seat was at the highest position in the courtroom. We entered a busy courtroom and the only familiar faces were the marshals and our court appointed attorneys. By this time we were overcome with fear. We were like fish out of water; our surroundings were unfamiliar, and we didn't know what to look for, or expect.

There was no trial because we entered a guilty plea to interstate transportation—driving a stolen car across the state line. So, all the judge had to do was pronounce sentence. To everyone's surprise the judge was sympathetic towards us. He gave us a lengthy lecture concerning our future if we continued to ignore the rules and laws of society. In those days your sentence immediately followed the verdict. After his lecture he was ready to pronounce sentence. He looked down from his lofty position and asked, "Young men, do either of you have anything to say before sentencing?"

I had prepared a speech in my head, but I was so fearful the only words I could utter were, "No, your Honor."

"My experience as a judge tells me I should give you both a stiff sentence," he said, "but my fatherly intuition tells me you both deserve another chance."

I glanced around the courtroom at the unfamiliar faces of the white spectators, and I actually saw contempt and scorn in their eyes for Jimmy and me, but I couldn't understand why.

"I am going to obey my intuition this time, and I hope it is a decision I will not regret. I am going to give you two that chance, and I want you to prove that I made the right decision by keeping your noses clean." He paused briefly and continued, "I sentence you both to two years probation; however, if either of you so much as stump your toe within two years, you will be brought back here and made to do those years in a federal institution. Is that understood?"

We looked toward the floor and replied, "Yes, your Honor."

I was so happy that I didn't know what to do; I couldn't believe it. We had another chance, but another chance to do what? To be good boys? To learn from our bad experience? To commit more serious crimes? Another chance to do what?

While we are still little children, we are already programmed for life. Half of the things we learn in life are already learned by the time we reach grade school. At times that programming is good, but often it is bad. We were only little boys in big bodies who had been programmed wrong somewhere along the line.

The marshals took us back to the county jail where we had to wait until all the necessary paper work was completed, and this took several days. But, I didn't care how long it took because I knew that I had another chance and was going home. When the papers were completed, we were taken to the Trailway Bus Station bound for Greensboro, North Carolina.

When I arrived home, my family was ecstatic, and everyone was so glad to see me, and I was so glad to be back home. I stayed home for awhile, but then I was back on the streets. I had been programmed all right; within two months I was arrested again in Winston Salem with a stolen car.

The state refused to prosecute me and I was transported back to Georgia for violating probation. What a fool I was; but crying wasn't going to help me now.

I was taken to the same county jail and back before the same federal judge. He looked at me with disappointment and sadness, and he had no other choice but to do what he did. He sentenced me to two years in the National Training School for Boys in Washington, D.C. I would never see Jimmy again, and it would be a long time before I saw home this time.

Now I was under the jurisdiction of the feds. I would be transported to Washington by automobile. Two marshals would take me as far as they were going in my direction and drop me off in a county jail. I would stay there several days or a week before I was picked up by other marshals going in my direction. This seemed to take forever because they were not permitted to travel after dark.

The practice of imprisoning people for crimes against society is as old as history. Before the era of imprisonment, convicted criminals were punished in a variety of cruel ways. If you were convicted of a serious crime, or in some instances not so serious, you were subjected to the penalty by methods such as crucifixion, poisoning, drowning, or burning at the stake.

Later in our history, we were no longer considered barbarians, so we invented other methods of discipline. Now we used more humane techniques for punishment like hanging, shooting, beheading, and electrocution. Another form of punishment that was used before imprisonment was transporting criminals to far and distant lands, and many European countries resorted to this practice. As far back as 1897, Great Britain had a law calling for deportation to America. Great Britain deported convicted felons to Gibraltar and Australia; Russia to Siberia; France to Devil's Island and other locations.

In short, prior to the use of prisons, convicted offenders were subjected to a wide variety of physical punishment, and they were all designed with one purpose in mind, to make them suffer. In 1959, all the emphasis was still on punishment, and very little was said about rehabilitation. Little did I know then that conditions would get worse, not better.

My first stop or layover was in Macon, Georgia. It was the largest jail I had ever seen at the time. It was four or five tiers high with four bunks to a cell made in a circular shape. I had never seen anything like it, and the noise was deafening. I think because of my age they didn't place me immediately in a cell on the tier. Instead, I was placed in an area in the back; it was a huge cell, and I didn't have a cell mate.

The cell adjacent to mine was occupied by a white youth about my age. We quickly became acquainted and spent long hours at our door talking late into the night. He even introduced me to his family, and when they brought him homemade food they shared it with me. Whenever they visited him, they would call me to the door and I would spend time in conversation with them.

Early one morning they took me from my cell and placed me in a cell on one of the tiers. To this day, I will always believe the only reason they moved me was because he was white and I was black, and I was getting too close to him and his family. Remember, this was the state of Georgia, home of the KKK, and I had the wrong complexion. I hated to leave my new friend that I knew I would never see again.

The tier was strictly segregated and because of my age I realized I had to be cautious. Naturally I was afraid; perhaps there is nothing quite like a prison experience to unmask all that we are. The environment itself is unnatural, oppressive, and violent. It had no system to classify and house you according to age and the seriousness of your offense. Everyone was mixed together, the thieves with the murderers, the youth with the aged, and the good with the bad. If a cook put everything in a pot and stirred it up, the end results may be a good soup. But if you housed all these characters together, the end results is often a professional criminal.

We breed criminals that become more of a threat to society after they come out of prison than before they became a part of it. Thus, prisons become factories of crime. Society sends all the raw materials and the prisons mold them only to turn out an end product that has become wise in ways of committing future crimes with little or no remorse for victims.

So, here I was a piece of raw material being mixed into the pot. I began to take a part in the great play of life, and I began to live a lie. I acted tough, ultra slick, and played the rough guy roll. Little did I realize then that the cost would be devastating.

On the tier there wasn't much to do; we were locked in our cells at night, and during the day I walked the tier and watched the men gamble playing cards and checkers. They never got tired of asking me questions concerning the city, and what I didn't know I made up as I went along. They wanted to know about the pretty young girls, the latest dances and cars. Again, what I didn't know, I simply invented; I was too smart to admit I didn't know.

I remained there for several months before I moved on toward my destination. I would stay in almost a dozen other jails before I arrived in Washington. I rode mostly in silence with the fear of the unknown playing tricks on my mind.

The feds had many institutions that were normally referred to as prisons, houses of corrections, juvenile reform schools or correctional schools, reformatories for young male adults, reformatories for women, and penitentiaries. In 1876, Elmira Reformatory was opened to substitute for the penitentiary. Youthful offenders who violated federal laws were sent to reformatories or correctional schools. But soon after these institutions were created, many students admitted that very little improvement was possible in an institution that herds together large numbers of men who had found it difficult to accept the general customs of society. So even then, many recognized that prisons were a failure.

When we arrived in Washington, D.C., I couldn't believe my eyes; this was the first large city I had ever seen. The route the marshals took didn't allow me to see much, but it was enough. Immediately, I knew it was a beautiful city even though I wasn't a tourist.

From the front seat one of the marshals said, "Well son, this is it."

So, this was to be my home for the next two years. We were in the northeast section of the city at Blandensburg Road and South Dakota Avenue. There it set high upon a hill, but the sight was deceptive. The National Training School for Boys didn't look like a training school at all. The lawn was like a pretty green carpet surrounded with shrubbery. It had the appearance of a large college campus.

We drove up the long driveway and more buildings became visible as we stopped in front of the administration building and parked. Directly across from the administration building was the chapel, to its left was Franklin Hall and next to it was Edison. Almost directly behind Edison was Jefferson and next to that was the academic school. Setting in front of the school was the kitchen and in back were the vocational shops.

The marshals took me to the administration building and released me in their custody. Being that this was a federal training school, there were young adults from all over the United States ranging in ages from fourteen to eighteen; occasionally, there were a few twenty-one year olds. The population was made up of blacks, whites, Puerto Ricans, Cubans, and a handful of youths from Poland.

I was processed and taken to the admission building. Everyone was dressed in uniform khaki pants and shirts with brown boots or shoes. Naturally the majority of the population were blacks and they were from Washington, and they ruled the hill as it was called. Normally if you were not from Washington you were considered a bamma, not part of the in-crowd. It didn't take me long to be considered as part of the in-crowd. I began to act out the tough guy role I had played in the county jails. I did everything to be accepted by my peers. I was still searching, trying to find myself, but mostly I just wanted to belong. It didn't matter how bad they were or what they did; I just wanted to be a part of them.

The population was a deception also. We were a minority in the United States but a majority in terms of the prison population, so according to the population, black folks were the only ones committing crimes.

I made friends fast. I stayed in the admission building for thirty days, and then moved to Franklin Cottage and was assigned to work in the kitchen. I soon earned the nickname of "Cheese" and was part of the herd.

My grandparents and most of my mother's family had moved to Washington, so I fitted right in and this was my new home. Many of my friends would later make headlines for committing crimes of all sorts. Washington had the slickest and smoothest youngsters anywhere. Slick was their trademark; they were slick in their walk, talk, dance, and most of all their style of dress. They wore Dobb hats, cashmere top coats, gabardine slacks, and footjoy shoes. This was the style of dress for the teens as early as the '50s.

In retrospect, I thought I stood alone playing games, but we all were. At first we entered the field walking the yard, always looking over our shoulders in fear. We still had that fresh youthful look in our eyes but it wouldn't last long. We were young and carefree, but our hearts would become hardened by the masks we wore and the games we played. We thought the mask was our strength but it really was our weakness. We never stopped to think for one moment of the reasons we were here. We were only having fun, looking for an escape, and trying to find a release from the pressures of being young; none of our actions seemed that serious.

Many of us would probably never become what we could because of what changed us in here, and the masks we learned to wear, and the games we learned to play.

Shortly after I was in Franklin Cottage, and settled down, I stayed in trouble. I had one incident after another and spent a great deal of time in segregation, or in the hole as we called it. It was situated under the admission building. It had a small recreation room and small dorm with a dozen or so beds. It was reserved mostly for those who were being transferred to large and more adult prisons.

My first trip there was for fighting. I was stripped down to my shorts and given a j ump suit and put into one of the eight cells. The cell was totally bare with the exception of a small hole in the back of it that served as a toilet. The button to flush the toilet was located outside the cell, therefore you were forced to smell your own urine and defecation until the officers flushed it. They gave me a mat for a bed at night, but they took it every morning at five o'clock. They fed me the minimum amount of food, and after so many days they took me before the board to determine my status to see if they were going to release me back into population.

As much as I hated that hole, I just couldn't stay out for any length of time. I made my mother promises to stay out of trouble, promises that I never kept because I was too busy playing games and being a clown. Before long I somehow got used to it, but at first it was hell! When I heard the key turn that door and lock, I was horrified. I began to have claustrophobia. The walls seemed to close in on me and I had trouble breathing.

In the gray dawn of the morning, thoughts of my family were my only solace. What was my mother doing; did she know that I loved her although I rarely told her? What were my sister and brothers doing? Did they realize how much I missed them? I never thought I would miss hearing my sister scream, "I'm going to tell mommy on you." At night it seemed like I would die a thousand times between dusk and dawn. But I just couldn't understand why I kept coming back, why I continued to stay in trouble, and what it would take for me to learn.

To my surprise one afternoon, they called me to the control center. I was to see Captain McGee. I entered his office and he was sitting behind a desk. After I took a seat, he looked at me in silence for a long time, and then he spoke, "Son, I've been hearing a lot about you lately. Every time there is a disturbance or confusion, your name comes up."

I sat there without saying a word in defense.

He then opened a large manila folder and began to turn pages. After a brief moment he gave me a sympathetic look. "But, I don't see how in the world one man can do all they say you do."

For a moment I thought he saw through me, because what he was about to tell me would stay with me for a very long time.

Each Night, I Die

"Personally, I don't think you are a bad kid; most of our kids are not bad. Mischievous maybe, but not bad. I see so many of you youngsters that come here spending your time fighting for a reputation simply because you are afraid to be yourself. One day you will have to see yourself as you really are, and there will be nowhere for you to hide."

What is he talking about? I thought. Nothing could be farther from the truth, could it?

At last he said, "If I were you I would give some serious thought to what I just said."

I saw a concerned look in his eyes, a genuine look of concern, but I dismissed it because I had been educated by my friends that guards don't really care about prisoners. He needed to talk to his officers and tell them I wasn't a bad fellow. I thanked him for his lecture and returned to my cottage.

My mother would take time off from her job and visit me when she could from Greensboro. Her visits were twofold; her primary concern was to see me, but at the same time she could visit her family. Although my family always stood beside me, they never condoned my criminal wrongdoing.

On her visits, she arrived in the morning and stayed until the afternoon. I had mixed emotions on these visits. On one hand I was ecstatic. In her eyes I could clearly see the love she had for me as she told me about my sisters and brothers. But, beyond her eyes and smiles, I could see the hurt and pain I was causing her. I could see it, but not understand it. What did I know about love? I was just a stupid kid masquerading as a man. After a few days, she had to say farewell. I would kiss her goodbye and always promise to be better.

If your behavior was satisfactory, with the board's approval, you were permitted an eight-hour pass home the first Sunday of the month. An adult family member had to pick you up by eight in the morning and have you back by four. If you were out of state, you had to have a family member who was a resident of Washington to qualify for a pass.

All of my friends were making home visits, and I was determined to make one also. I was fed up hearing them return telling their fantastic lies, or maybe I was angry because I didn't have any lies to tell of my own.

I remember when Eddie stayed out of trouble long enough to make his first home visit. We had the record player out on the bench playing the latest hit records waiting for him to return. It was after four and we were worried.

"You don't think it got too good to him that he forgot how to tell time, do you?" I asked no one in particular.

Phillip stopped dancing long enough with his imaginary partner to respond, "If he did he better keep going."

When Eddie did get back he was almost an hour late and was grounded for a period of ninety days. He let everyone smell his breath so we would know that he had been drinking and his finger to prove he had been with a girl.

I felt left out because I didn't have any tales to tell, so I was determined to make a home visit. I stayed out of trouble and my cottage officers put me in for a visit. To everyone's surprise, I made it.

My aunt Polly's husband came to sign me out and I spent the day with them. They also took me to visit some other relatives I had never seen before. I had a wonderful time, and I went back to the school and told them all the things I thought they wanted to hear. I had no girlfriend, so I invented lies and boasted about my manhood.

Time for me began to pass rapidly and soon I was going for parole. I got the shock of my life when I made it; it was the talk of the hill. "Cheese was going home." It was the spring of 1962, and I was going home; I could not believe it. Close to two years had come and gone and I never thought once of what I was going to do when I got there. What could I do? I hadn't even learned a trade, but the federal government was sending me home with a smile.

I made my rounds and said goodbye to everyone. I had learned how to dress, dance, fight, and be slick, and I was headed back to Greensboro, N.C. The officers took me to the bus station and all I could see now was home sweet home!

6

Home Again

It was late afternoon in August, 1962 when I arrived back in Greensboro. I was seventeen, and all I could think of was trying to play catch up for the two years I had been away. I was much too immature to realize no man can redeem the time or call back yesterday.

My mother and sister were at the station to greet me. This was the first time that I had seen my sister in two years. She was a skinny little buck-toothed girl when I left; now she was all grown up. She rushed over, grabbed me around the neck and began to plant kisses all over my face.

"Don't smother him to death," my mother had to tell her. She was making so much noise I thought we would get arrested for disturbing the peace. Our family had a matriarchal structure, but we functioned as well as any two parent household.

We took a local taxi home. We were living on Best Street at the time. When the taxi stopped in front of the house, Daisy leaped out first and began to scream again, "My brother is home; my brother is home." Their next door neighbors and best friends came out and joined her in celebration. Their name was the Shaws, and they, too, were a one-parent household. It consisted of the mother and three daughters; two of the girls were my age. I stood checking the two oldest girls out and looking them over closely. Daisy quickly introduced us as if she was reading my dirty mind.

It was an attractive neighborhood, and most of the neighbors were friendly. These homes were recently built for low income families and most were headed by single parents. They had two levels and were built essentially the same.

Mom was still working hard to support us, and the house was spic-and-span. The floors were waxed and polished. The furniture was mostly new and modem, and everything was neatly arranged. I was overwhelmed. I stood in amazement and wondered how she could do it all alone.

On the surface it appeared that everything had changed. The street gangs had disbanded and there was no more gang fighting. Little girls had become young ladies. Some friends had entered the military because there were no jobs and nothing else to do after they graduated from school, but a few would make a name for themselves. Louis (Sweet Lou) Hudson would become a star with the Atlanta Hawks, Fred (Curly)

Neal would become a star with the international Harlem Globetrotters, Charlie and Inez Fox would record hit songs and become stars in the music industry, and I stood trapped in the past, wondering where time had gone and trying to call back yesterday.

But beneath the surface I saw that some things never changed. Mom continued to work hard every day. She continued to put her children before herself. She continued to struggle and do the best she could with what she had, and not once did I hear her complain. But above all, she continued to love us with a deep and profound love.

But something or someone was missing; a family member was absent. Where was my little brother? Why wasn't he here to greet me? Now it was time for them to break the bad news.

"Junior," mom said, "we didn't tell you because we thought it was best to wait, because we didn't want to upset you."

I really didn't know what to expect; I mean, what could be so terrible?

"He stopped going to school, and every time we turned around he was in some kind of trouble with the law, so the judge finally had to send him to training school. But, he'll be back home next year."

Junior was the name my family had given to me when I was small, and I didn't particularly like for anyone else to call me that but them. I guess Daisy thought it was a good time to give me some sisterly advice because she joined in.

"You should try to set a better example for him. Haven't you noticed whatever you do, good or bad, he is only a step behind?"

"I never thought about it, Sis," and I hadn't.

With great concern she said, "Well, now is the time."

I promised her I would, but I had gotten in the habit of making promises that I couldn't keep. I saw my old friend Doug, but for some reason we were no longer friends. When I did see him, we talked for a few minutes and went our separate ways. I felt out of tune sitting around the house. For two years, I had been told when to eat, when to sleep, when to talk, and when to work. I was full of energy and excitement and ready to go. Soon I was back on the streets and everything was back to normal.

My first real girlfriend's name was Nancy. Every night after consuming cheap bottles of wine, I went to Arts. It was my favorite dance hall and place to hang out at night, and it was there that I met her. I wish I could say she was the loveliest girl that I had ever seen, but I can't. Physical beauty she didn't have; she was just an average looking girl. Yet, there was something about her that called out the beast in me. She was four or five years my senior and already had one child, and she made me feel like a grown man whose part I was busy playing.

Instantly, I realized she was not like any girlfriend I ever had. One night after spending the night with her, I got home that morning and found mom preparing to go to work. Daisy had already begun her daily chores.

As soon as I came through the door mom said, "Where have you been boy? You can get into some more trouble if you want to; don't call me."

I thought to myself, "Here she goes preaching again."

"As a matter of fact, you should think about what you are going to do with your life, or do you plan on running the streets all your life?"

"Where have you been sleeping?" Daisy asked. "Mommy," she screamed, "Look at his clothes; it looks like he's been sleeping in a lint factory."

"I bet you had better mind your business, girl!"

"You are my business; you're my brother."

What could I say? I knew that they loved me with all their hearts and wanted to see me do the right thing.

It didn't take long before everyone knew that Nancy and I were going steady. I really didn't have that much experience with girls prior to her. Of course, there were girls, but she was my first serious relationship; it took her to make me realize how much I had been missing. While Nancy worked, I hung out in the streets drinking wine and seeing how mischievous I could be. Naturally, when mom and sis found out about Nancy, they both hit the ceiling. They were familiar with her, and they gave me a lengthy lecture.

"Don't you think you should be going steady with a girl more you own age?" mom wanted to know.

My smart mouth sister couldn't wait. "Yea, she is old enough to be his mommy, she got babies, and plus she is ugly."

"She got one kid."

"That's all you know about."

"If they paid you for signifying, you would be rich."

I could tell where this conversation was leading so I stormed out of the house, but not before I heard her say, "Run! You never could stand the truth."

Erik Erikson, the noted psychologists, said that in the developmental process of each adolescent he reaches a stage where he must move in a positive or negative direction. I was searching for an identity and a sense of knowing just where I was going. I developed a deviant identity and life style that stayed at odds with the values and expectations of society. My generation rejected most of the dominant values of our previous generation. They had their day, and we declared the '50s to be ours.

I began to drink more and more. One drink wasn't enough and two was too many. Alcohol had a violent and destructive effect upon me. I would lose complete control and have brief episodes of blackouts. I knew I couldn't handle it, but I continued to drink. It was a problem that I would later compound and lead to my total destruction.

I attempted to pack two days into every 24 hours; I was living like there was no tomorrow. Nancy could no longer satisfy my carnal and bestial lust, so I began to see other girls more my age. I still had to be careful because Nancy was not only possessive, she was also very jealous.

My sister had a girlfriend named Edna who lived on the next block. She was small, beautiful, and attractive. She was completely different from the girls I had been seeing and dating; she was a good girl and I didn't want to ever hurt her. Many years later I would still carry a torch for her, and I'd lie in prison cells dreaming and fantasizing about her. "Edna," I would silently call her name over and over again, "why can't we bring back our yesterdays?"

She was strikingly beautiful. She had a golden brown complexion and stood just about five feet tall. She had long black wavy hair and keen features, and she had a habit of looking at me with those beautiful eyes that seemed to pierce my very soul. Somehow, I could never bring myself to tell her how I really felt about her. She was a good girl, and I didn't think that I was good enough for her. At times I dreamed about flying away with her, living forever in her love. But, "if" is a word of 50 million, and still I would not have been good enough for her. Despite all that I felt for her, she was the one girl that I could never have.

Edna rarely went to dances, and for her to attend a party was almost unheard of. The total of her time was spent at home when she wasn't in school. When I came home from the training school, she suddenly began to visit my sister on somewhat of a regular basis, and I found myself knocking at her door pretending to see her brother, especially when I thought she was home alone.

One afternoon, dead tired and weary from running the streets, I was enjoying a quiet moment at home alone when I heard a knock at the door. She stood there, and my heart leaped in my chest. Before I could speak, I opened the screen door and she came in.

"Where is Daisy?" she asked.

"I really don't know, Edna, but she should be back soon."

"Is it all right if I wait for her?"

I observed her closely, and for some strange reason, I sensed that she was a little nervous. "Of course, you can wait."

We sat down on the sofa and began to talk; we talked about school and other minor affairs; then our conversation became serious.

"Is Nancy still your girlfriend?" she wanted to know.

I wanted to lie, but I didn't. "I still see her every now and then." I moved closer to her on the sofa, and my hand found its way to her small and luscious knee. I waited for her to pull away but she didn't.

Stop Cheese! Stop! My conscience screamed; there is an invisible line that will always separate you from her. I came as close as I ever would to crossing that imaginary line in the next several minutes.

"Cheese, I think I lie awake until you come home every night," she said, looking at me with her pretty dark brown eyes.

"But, how do you know when I come home, Edna?" What was she trying to say? I realized how hard it was for her to say that, but did her statement need further interpretation.

"I know what time you come home almost every night. I hear your footsteps on the sidewalk, and I can tell it's you. When I hear that walk, I look out the window and sure enough it is always you. Then, I can lie down and go to sleep because I know you are home safe."

I removed my hand from her knee, and took a lock of her beautiful hair and rubbed it between my forefinger and thumb. And as gently as I possibly could, I kissed her on her lips. At that moment, nothing else in the whole world seemed to matter. And my mind exploded into a thousand fragments. When my mind returned to earth, my mother had entered the house. She got my attention by making a deep throaty sound with her voice.

"Hi, Edna," she said as she went directly upstairs.

"Hello, Mrs. Cheese." I could tell she was embarrassed. She thought she had committed some grave sin because mom had caught us necking. We looked at each other for what seemed like a long time. In my head I searched for words that would not come, so she never would know of the feelings that I had for her buried deep within my soul. Soon she got up and headed for the door. I told her I would see her when she got home from school the next day. But promises, promises, I never could keep.

When mom came down stairs, she asked, "Where is Edna?"

"She just went home." When I told her that, I thought I detected a sign of disappointment in her. Edna was her kind of girl.

I continued to stay in the streets committing petty crimes; I never gave a minute's thought to the consequences of my action. One night my partner and I were on our way home when I thought our careers had come to an end. We were both intoxicated, driving in from one of the nearby counties. He had dozed off to sleep and I was getting drowsy from the lack of sleep and too much cheap wine. I must have dozed momentarily because when I opened my eyes, I was in a state of shock.

My eyes opened to hear a loud scratching sound, and I saw red hot particles flying into the air. I was driving across a long bridge and the right side of the car was scraping the side of the bridge. I had fallen asleep behind the wheel and lost control.

My partner opened his eyes in complete horror, "What the-?"

I fought to regain control, ignoring his remarks.

"What are you trying to do, kill us!"

When I gained control, I took a deep breath. "That was close," I tried to say with humor, but neither of us were laughing.

In 1962, everything caught up with me at once. Nancy and I had a big fight after she caught me with another girl.

Edna started going study with a lawbreaker, and I was waiting to be tried for auto theft and carrying a deadly weapon.

Because of the seriousness of the offenses, mom scraped and borrowed money and hired me an attorney. He was a retired judge and highly respected. He assured me he was going to do all that he could to see that I got the least amount of time for the charges, but still, I was afraid and didn11 know what to expect.

Soon the day arrived for me to stand before another judge who would determine if I would go to prison, and for how long. My attorney was good at his word because when I heard the sentence I couldn't believe it. I was sentenced to six months on the road camp with a stipulation that when I completed my sentence I would leave the state of North Carolina. But, this was to be a hard six months.

After sentencing, I was immediately transferred to a camp a short distance beyond the city limits. It was a small camp with a small population. The camp included a few scattered buildings surrounded by a tall fence. One of the buildings housed the entire population; it was a large plain building made into two dormitories separated by a narrow hall. The majority of prisoners were from Charlotte, N.C. and Greensboro.

The single thing that I hated most about this camp was the hard work. Shortly after breakfast, five days a week, we lined up in the yard according to our working squads. Each squad had a number. When your squad number was called by the captain, you got aboard a truck that was nothing more than a large cage and went to work. It was hot in the summer and cold in the winter. We dug ditches, cut the bushes alongside the highways, tar-patched roads, and whatever else was assigned to us. We came back to camp at noon for lunch and went back to work until late afternoon. I never worked so hard in my life. Within a few days, I had large blisters on both hands from using picks, shovels, and axes. I'd be dead tired and beat every afternoon when we returned to camp. I would not work in the street if you paid me, but I had to work in prison for no wages at all.

I remember on weekends, mom would visit, and I would be glad to see her and hear the news from home. She had a better paying job and my brother was on his way back home. At night, I would lie awake and think about Nancy, Edna, and a few other girls I had known. Nancy had another man. Edna was pregnant, and her boyfriend had recently been killed.

One Sunday I was called for a visit. I was sure it was mom, but she also had Daisy and Edna with her. They told me Nancy was spreading rumors that we were going to get married when I came home. We all got a big laugh out of that. Mom and sis said goodbye and I had a few minutes with Edna alone.

"Edna," I said to her, "you still look as lovely as ever." I waited for her to speak, but she was silent. There was so much I wanted to say to her to try to make her understand. I wanted to say, "Edna, a flame burns within my soul for you, a fire and heat that no one has been able to smother. It is you I dream of at night when everyone else is asleep; it is your voice I hear ringing in my ears and knocking upon the door of my heart." I wanted to speak, I tried to tell her, but somehow I couldn't. Instead, I said, "Although I could never tell you, you've always meant the world to me."

When I looked away, I heard her say, "Then, why did you always hide it?" Her voice was full of tenderness, warmth, and passion.

"Because, Edna, I never thought I was good enough for you."

"And, I didn't think I was good enough for you." Slowly, tears fell from her lovely eyes, and our visit ended. I went to bed that night and cried, "Edna, oh Edna, why can't we call back yesterday?"

About two weeks later I was released. Mom had made the necessary arrangements for me to live in Washington with one of her sisters. She was sure if I changed location and environment, I would stay out of trouble. I came home from camp on Thursday, and Friday mom took me to the bus station bound for Washington, D.C.; it was like going back home.

I had said good-bye to Greensboro for the last and final time. I never saw Nancy again. Years later, I would see Edna in Washington on her way to New York. On my many trips to the city, I would go to see her on several occasions. But, even to this day, she never understood how much I really felt for her. You see, we were never able to call back YESTERDAY.

7

The Promised Land

"Black folks are the last people in the world who ought to commit crimes, because when they get caught, they know they are not going to get a fair shake."

Dick Gregory

It was mid-summer in 1962 when I arrived back in Washington, and this was to be my Promised Land. When I first came here two years ago, I was a federal prisoner, but now I was returning a free man. It was as though I had never seen the city before, and in reality, I hadn't. When I went out on eight-hour passes from the training school, I had only seen a small portion of northeast Washington. I was not aware that the city was divided into four sections, and northeast was only a small part of the whole.

It was as if the city and its inhabitants had changed overnight. But the city hadn't changed; it was my outlook, vision, and perspective that had changed. I was viewing the city no longer as an adolescent, and I saw for the first time another portion of the city.

When I entered the bus terminal it was late at night, and I stood for a moment and surveyed my Promised Land as if I was a viewer observing the world on a giant screen. I saw a large mass of people rushing toward some unknown destination. There were a host of suspicious characters lurking in the shadows of the dark, there were shot players busy on the prowl, and there were fakes looking for easy marks. Prostitutes came and left in pairs, looking for customers to satisfy their greedy and brutal pimps, and drug addicts stood looking off into space as the whole world passed them by. And, I heard an echo in my ear saying, "Look! this is your long lost Promised Land."

I didn't enter the city in chains, but I was more of a prisoner now than I was two years ago. The chains I wore were not visible; nevertheless, I was a prisoner just the same. My soul was bound in chains. I was still in search of who I was, and I was becoming bitter by the day. At times I struggled to break free from captivity to free my soul, but at other times I was content to remain a prisoner not by force, but by choice. I was too young and immature to understand that only I could determine what I was to become, not the environment, conditions, or circumstance.

I telephoned my mother's sister, and she came to pick me up at the bus terminal. She was a nurse and had a large house in northeast Washington. This was the same aunt who took me out on eight-hour passes from the training school. When she didn't come, her husband came to get me. They had four children: Gwen, Tony, Rose Mary, and Ernie. Although I loved them and they treated me like a member of their family, I didn't stay there long.

I later moved in with my mother's youngest sister and husband. It appeared to me that everyone was writing me off as a bad risk; I think they thought that I would always be a hoodlum. It was never verbalized, but I always felt it. May, as everyone called her, was more of my generation, and this was the motivating factor that caused me to move in with her. I could discuss matters with her that I didn't dare discuss with others.

Until this time, I was unfamiliar with this section of the city; they were living at 1st and K Street Northwest. I had grown accustomed to the rather quiet residential section of the northeast, but northwest

Washington had a reputation for being the major attraction of the entire city. There was the White House, Washington Monument, Smithsonian Institution, Museum of Art, and a host of other world famous tourist attractions. But, there was also 14th and T, 7th and T, 9th and O, and 9th and U Street. It's the heart of the inner city; this is where thousands upon thousands went to bed at night to open their eyes in the morning, attempting to relieve the plastic dreams they had dreamed in the night, artificial dreams that could never be real. This is the part of the city where you could be anything you wanted to be that was not employable.

This is a section of the city where education meant being street smart, where wisdom was designed and frowned upon, and ignorance was admired.

The white folks had left the inner city to black folks, and we had come in large numbers and raised our flag as if we were conquers of the Promised Land. I was a rebellious youth; I was rebelling against a society that I felt was oppressive and unfair. Every time we demanded equality, they had a way of telling us to slow down and cool the engine. I was rebellious because I hated the contradiction in its system of laws. Fresh in my mind was the Blue Law that made it illegal to sell alcoholic beverages on Sunday, but it was perfectly legal to lynch a black man for sport, and leave his body hanging on a tree like a strange piece of fruit. I rebelled because it had one law for the rich and another for the poor, one was justice and the other justice deferred. I rebelled because it was always right, and I was made to feel wrong no matter what I did.

I was learning to hate everything that was not like me. I found it much easier to hate than to try to love and understand. At first I hated everyone whose skin was not the same as mine. Then, I hated those whose views were at odds with mine. Soon I was hating everyone because subconsciously I hated myself. I hated myself because I felt worthless; I was uneducated, poor, and jobless.

At first I looked for legal employment and found it. I went to an employment agency and they secured me a job washing dishes. What else could I do with a criminal record and an eighth-grade education? The agency was paid a percentage of my pay for four weeks for their service. I worked hard six days a week. Every Friday when I was paid, I cashed my check, paid rent, purchased clothes, and brought home a twenty-five dollar money order and put it under my mattress. For some reason I had developed a habit of saving; maybe it was out of fear of not knowing what tomorrow would bring.

Soon I was back on the street hanging out. I was getting a much closer look at the inner city. Every day after work I rushed home, bathed, changed clothes, and headed straight for 14th and Harvard Street. Sometimes I would be in too much of a hurry to go home first, so I would go directly to my destination. All of my old friends were coming home from the training school, and we were all hanging out. There was Rob, Fats, Sammy, and a multitude of others. We went to all the parties, drank wine, ran the streets, and lived as if there was no tomorrow. I could no longer work and run the streets, so I gave up my dishwashing job for the streets.

Without a job and no income, Rob and I began to commit crimes to support our lifestyles. The inner city had always had an extremely high crime rate, and I've always had my own theory as to the reason why. Most blacks subconsciously had an inferiority complex as far as committing crimes in the white neighborhoods; when they went beyond their own environment, they no longer had that air of confidence; consequently, the crimes they committed were in their own environment and neighborhood. And we contributed to the increase in the crime statistics in the inner city.

One night Rob and I committed a small robbery on a grocery store. When we came out of the store, in haste, I put the shotgun in a brown paper bag. As we approached the exit to the alley, I put the gun underneath my right arm with the barrel pointing toward the ground.

A few feet from the exit, "BOOM", a loud blast exploded from the bag. I leaped four feet in the air, and before my feet touched the pavement, Rob had darted out the alley and around the corner. He thought it was the police firing at us. I forgot I had pulled the trigger back on the shotgun in the store and left it in that position. I was extremely lucky I didn't blow my leg completely off.

Sunday afternoon the place to be was Odd Fellows. It was located on 9th Street, and everyone gathered here to dance and show off. If you wanted to know who was who, all you had to do was show up at Odd Fellows on Sunday afternoon. Everyone came here to exhibit to the crowd how well they were doing. We styled in the latest fashions, flashed our small bank rolls, boasted about our last great achievement, and tried to impress upon the cute young girls that we were the future successes of tomorrow.

On one of my earliest visits an extremely attractive young girl caught my attention. She had on tight pants with a big butt, and her name was Cindy. Rob introduced us, and I asked her to dance; she was definitely my kind of girl. I spent most of the evening with her dancing and talking, and I told her I was looking forward to seeing her the following Sunday.

I moved from my aunt's to 15th and R Street Northwest; this was the first place I had of my very own. I had clothes in my closet, a few dollars in my pocket, and a date with Cindy on Sunday. And to me, the Promised Land never looked better.

Sunday, when I arrived at Odd Fellows, I didn't have any trouble locating her. I had come alone. I left Rob behind because he had met a new girl and he couldn't let her go. Cindy had a small crowd with her, and they looked at me in suspense as I approached them. When I reached them, I took Cindy's hand with confidence and led her out on the dance floor.

Every time they played a slow record we danced and talked. I really got to know her, and I liked her very much. She was full of fire and spunk. That night when we left, I walked her home like a school boy. She was still in school and two years younger than me. We sat on her steps talking for hours getting to know each other even better. A car stopped in front of the house and a lovely young woman got out. It was her mom. After she introduced us, I immediately liked her.

"Cindy, don't stay out much longer because you have school in the morning," her mom said as she entered the house.

To remain on good terms with her mom, I kissed her good night on her lips. I asked her to be my girl, and somewhat to my surprise, she said yes. To prove I was a big fellow, before I left, I gave her some money and told her to buy something pretty for me.

"What are you going to buy with it?"

"You'll see."

"I'm sure l will," I said, leaving with a smile on my face.

Finally, my family arrived in Washington. I was never so glad to see them in my life. Mom and Daisy got jobs, but I kept taking chances in the streets trying to be a hustler. Soon, my brother followed me to the streets and began to make a name for himself. My mother, sister, and youngest brother didn't like northwest. They tried several locations before completely abandoning northwest for the quiet and peaceful section of southeast.

Every afternoon after school I would spend time with Cindy. I was very popular with her mother and sister. One day Cindy asked where I lived. When I told her I had a place of my own, she didn't believe it. Every day, she asked when I was going to take her to see it. After several failed promises, she began to seriously doubt that I had a place of my own.

When I chose the day to take her, I telephoned her and told her to be ready when I picked her up.

"Where are we going?"

"Just be ready when I get there," I told her.

When I got there she was very excited, although she didn't know where we were going. I flagged a taxi and gave the driver the address. She looked puzzled. After keeping her in suspense long enough, I told her; but still she didn't believe it. She was still in doubt.

She was silent as we climbed the stairs to the second floor. I opened the door with my key, and she slowly went ahead of me. When I closed the door, I leaned against the wall in silence.

"Cheese, who lives here?"

"I live here." I still couldn't understand why she didn't believe me. I led her to my closet and opened the door. Only after she saw my clothes did she finally believe me. And for the first time she completely relaxed. She stepped out on the small balcony and looked at the view.

"This is nice," she said as she came back into the bedroom. She had an odd look on her face; her eyes were aglow, and she slowly unbuttoned her blouse. "Look what your money bought." And she leaped into my bed.

I just couldn't believe it; red was my favorite color for girls. It was late night when I took her back home.

One night I went out hustling alone. Rob was with Gloria. She was a well-proportioned, voluptuous young lady with big legs and an extra big butt. Rob had developed a habit recently of falling in love every other week. Until his yearning and passion subsided, you couldn't get him out of bed if the house was on fire.

I took this night to burglarize a house I had been observing for some time. It was late at night when I made my unlawful entrance. I was sure the house was deserted. I was taking only the things of value that I could carry, but when I reached the second floor, I heard a familiar sound. It was the faint sound of someone snoring. I almost went into a state of panic. I was overcome with fright, and I didn't know exactly what to do. Should I run or stay? Be calm, I told myself; pull yourself together. As quickly as my fear came, it disappeared and my confidence was back. After loading my bag to its maximum capacity, I was ready to leave. As I made my exit, I was blinded by a beam of bright light shining directly in my face.

"Don't move an inch," I heard a voice from the darkness, "if you do you're dead."

I couldn't see, but there was no need to; I knew I was busted.

I had been guilty of committing a variety of foolish crimes, but now I was captured. While I was on a rampage, I never once gave thought to the consequence of my actions; we never do.

Black people should run from crime, but many of us don't. In many instances it has to do with economics and it is the only way out of a system that is overburdened and unjust. But that was not my case. I was guilty, caught in the act of committing a felony, but in the process I would meet a huge number of prisoners denying their guilt. Consequently, they came away fighting the system, bitter, angry, and bewildered because they didn't receive a fair trial. But, this was like wearing a blindfold. Did we really have to be apprehended to realize this naked truth? I did and a multitude of others did also.

The officers took me to the nearest district precinct and charged me with burglary and grand larceny. Early the next morning everyone arrested that night was transported to court for arraignment. We waited in large holding cells beneath the court for our names to be called to make our appearance before the judge. The judge heard the charges, set bail, and a date for preliminary hearing.

If you couldn't make bail, you were transported to the district jail, located at 200 19th Street Southeast. It was a huge dirty red structure with a tall fence which had rolls of wire on top. It resembled an ancient castle from a horror movie from out of the past.

This is the route that most of us took because we couldn't make bail. Whatever the bail amount was you had to pay ten percent or sign a property bond. A vast majority were considered lucky if they could make a thousand dollar bond and that was about as low as they came. If we had money in our pocket, we wouldn't have to commit crimes.

I couldn't make bail; no one was aware that I was arrested, so that afternoon I was in the large number that was transported to the jail. We were ushered off the old antiquated bus into the jail. All you could hear was the deafening sounds of electric gates opening and closing. As the guard in the control center announced your name, you stepped up to the window and he compared each incoming prisoner with his mug-shot photograph.

From there we were taken to R and D (Receiving and Diagnostic) where each man was processed. Usually this was a long and tiring process. We had to wait in cages with steel benches. We all had been up since 5 a.m. and now we just wanted to see a bunk.

If we were lucky, at about 7 p.m. we were ready to be processed. This procedure was performed by prisoners waiting to be tried, waiting to be transferred to Lorton, or serving small sentences in the jail. Although the guards supervised, all such positions were performed by prisoners.

As the prisoner called our names, we stepped from the holding cell into the receiving area. Prisoners were busy doing a variety of different jobs. We stripped completely and placed our clothes on a long table. The guard stood at the end with a wooden box with a lock on it. If you had money he placed it in the box and gave you a receipt. Then the prisoners behind the table went to work.

"Cheese, next man." One of the prisoners called my name.

I moved to the table and put down on the table all of my belongings and then moved back a step.

An older prisoner picked up each article and said in a loud voice, "He got brown up and brown down; he got brown on the ground."

Then, another prisoner asked, "How much he got?"

"Mark him 35," the older one said.

This meant that I had on a brown shirt, pants, and shoes; and I had thirty-five dollars in cash. The next procedure was more simple but much more humiliating.

"Step back," the voice of a third prisoner said.

I did what I was told as they shouted commands. "Raise your arms, run your fingers through your hair, open your mouth, and lift your tongue."

I was disgusted but I obeyed. If you play, you got to pay.

The commands went on. "Turn around; lift your feet; bend over and spread your cheeks."

"Next man," another voice said.

They gave me my underwear, socks, and shoes, then directed me down a flight of stairs to the shower. They sprayed me with a liquid for lice and crabs, and I took a shower and went back upstairs.

Once back upstairs, they issued me a cotton shirt and pants. Your charge and amount of bail usually determined what section of the jail you were assigned. It had four sections: CB-1, CB-2, CB-3, and a large and small dormitory. I was fingerprinted and given a number. I was considered a big boy now and my little burglary charge wasn't even considered serious, so I was assigned to the big dorm.

The large group of incoming prisoners who had come with me were now being separated. Some went to CB-1; some went to CB-2; and others went with me.

When I reached the dorm, a prisoner sitting behind a desk gave me a blanket and two sheets and assigned me a bunk. He was in his 30s and I could tell he had been around. Plus, they didn't give these positions to just anyone.

It was a huge dorm and had four rows of double bunks; it was packed to its capacity and in an uproar. I looked for a familiar face but didn't see one. I was alert and afraid because I wasn't sure what the next minute would bring.

When I reached my bunk, I saw familiar faces and a few friends from training school. These same faces I would see over and over again. Year after year, those who were lucky did not die from drugs and violence.

But this was my generation; we were a generation of youth who had dropped out of school and dropped out of life. We had no real concept of life and death, nor did we know what was real or counterfeit. We sacrificed short term pleasures for long-term pain. We had a negative image of ourselves, so we played games of death attempting to be something we could never be. But, this was my generation; we were 6 percent of the nation's population, but 45 percent of the population in prisons. We were children beginning to have children that were contributing to the delinquency rate, and 6 out of 10 babies were born to single mothers.

This was my generation, a generation of black men who had a larger population in prisons than on college campuses. We were ten times likely to die of murder than a white man and one out of six under the age of thirty-five was unemployed. YES, this was my generation but something terrible had gone wrong. We had been programmed wrong somewhere along the road.

Was it the school system? The high school dropout rate was 23 percent, and that percent got higher in proportion to the poor and minorities (35 percent for blacks and 45 percent for Hispanics). Some systems in large cities had rates as high as 52 percent of youths not graduating from high school.

Was it the school system where the principals and teachers didn't live in the neighborhood? Was it the school system with its middle class bias, where the schools were built for upper and middle class youngsters, staffed by the middleclass, and modeled after them, giving little or no consideration for the poor and minorities?

Was it educational self-fulfilling prophecies, where the children failed to learn because those who were charged with teaching them did not believe they would learn, did not expect them to learn, and did not act toward them in ways that would help them to learn?

Perhaps, it was religion, where the ministers preached the gospel on Sundays to the righteous, but they never took their God home with them because the things they did at home they knew He would not approve. Was it because they kept their God locked in a building, compromising the word because they were afraid to offend? Was it because they said the church was dead and all it needed was a grave song?

Was it the family, where a whole generation of babies were having babies? Was it because the black male youth thought his manhood was the size of his penis and how many babies he could make, and that welfare was a bonus gift? Was it because we had been told, and come to believe, we were fools and would fail in each of our attempts? Was it the environment we created for our young that produced nothing but violence and destruction?

This was my generation, a generation of youth who had adopted deviant behavior as an accepted way of life. What had happened to the school, church, and family? Once these proud social institutions had kept us together as a unit for generations; now they were deteriorating fast with the rising of each morning sun.

Mom and Daisy came to visit regularly. Contact visits were not permitted. I had to sit on a long row of booths with a small window with a telephone to speak through. I could sense they were terrified each time they came. Having to see me under those conditions was almost too much for them to bear. Although they attempted to conceal it, I could clearly see them sitting there in discomfort, simply because their love for me was so great.

When I went to court, my charges were reduced from a felony to a misdemeanor because I entered a guilty plea. Because I had pled guilty and saved the government the expense of a trial, I was only sentenced to one year. On the surface, a plea bargain would appear to be in favor of the defendant, but nothing could be further from the truth.

The Eighth Amendment prohibits excessive bail and the Supreme Court has ruled that the only function of bail was to help guarantee that the defendant would appear in court. But in most cases bail is often used against a defendant under the pretense of protecting the community or teaching him a lesson.

Most people have limited knowledge of how the legal system works and they would be surprised to know that there are almost no criminal trials in the United States. Seventy percent (over ninety percent in many states) of the defendants plead guilty, thus eliminating the need for a trial. So, most defendants cop a plea of guilty to a lesser offense than the one with which he was originally charged. What they do is charge a defendant with more crimes than actually took place to force him to plead guilty.

For example, a man may be charged with murder in the first degree, murder in the second degree, carrying a dangerous weapon, use of a hand gun, and a host of other charges stemming from the murder. If he takes a chance and goes to trial and is convicted on each count, he may never get out of prison. Instead, the court will offer him a lesser charge—from first degree to second degree—where the accused can plead guilty on the spot. To him there is a big difference between life for first degree and thirty years for second.

I've seen many men cop a plea regardless of whether they are guilty or not. They may be innocent of all charges, but they will plead guilty to a lesser charge before they take the risk of a trial that nine times out of ten will result in a conviction, especially if they are black and poor. In my case, I too, probably would plead guilty even if I had been innocent of all charges.

When I got back to the jail, I told my friends I had copped a plea, and they were not surprised because most of them had done or would do, the exact same. Several weeks later, I was transferred to Occquan, Virginia.

Occquan was located south of Washington and housed prisoners from the District who had been convicted of misdemeanors. Directly across the highway was the Women's prison; a mile or so down the road was Lorton Youth Center and Lorton Reformatory. This was a section of Virginia that was saturated with prisons for convicted criminals from the District of Columbia.

Occquan itself was a wide open complex without walls or a fence. It had twelve dormitories that were separated by a small beautiful yard. The main jobs were the kitchen, laundry, brickyard, and the farm. I was assigned to 6 Dorm and worked on the farm. The work was hard, but after one month I became the water boy; my job was to make sure the water can was full at all times and the remaining time I spent lying underneath a shade tree.

Now, my friends were much older and hardened criminals, and I spent my time learning how to be a better criminal upon release. Society cried it was much too costly to pour money into the system to make it work, so prisons served the function of breeding criminals who came out worse than they were when they first went in. My mentor was Fly Charles, and he was my idol and the one I wanted to be like. How sad it was, but these were the role models on whom we patterned our lives and sacrificed all that we had to become. We were unaware of our proud, rich African culture; no one told us we were descendants of kings and queens and royal black blood. So, I spent my time trying to become like Fly Charles because he was the man of the hour; he had a reputation, girls, money, and was esteemed by his peers. I came to love this man like a big brother I never had. Many nights, he and I lie awake until day break with him instructing me on the finer points of criminal activities.

My year had almost expired, and I was getting close to my release date when I met another con whose advise I would remember for some time to come. His name was Bill and he spent a lifetime on the streets. He was aware that Fly was polishing me for the street, so he pulled me aside one day and tried to show me the other side of the coin.

"Youngblood," he asked one day, "how old are you?"

I tried to say with as much pride as I could muster, "18, Bill."

"Yea, you're 18 going on 40, but you have your whole life ahead of you, Youngblood, and you still have a chance; don't spend what you got left looking for a Promised Land."

He was talking to me as if he was talking to a son. He was only in his 50s, but his head was full of white hair. "I'm a soldier, and I've been on the battlefield a long time, and I fought—fought real hard. I fought when there was no need to fight; I even fought when there was no one to fight but myself, but I kept on fighting; and for what?"

He paused and looked around and waved his black hand in the air, "All of this… for money, for freedom, for peace?" He took a breath and his face was as serious as I had ever seen him. His eyes became large as if he was giving a speech that his very life depended on.

"Youngblood, yesterday we fought to stay alive, fought for survival, fought to get ahead; but today, we are fighting for a cause that is locked deep inside our heads, but it was never just. Today, you are fighting the same war that I fought all my life. But you know what, Youngblood, I think you know today, just as I've known all my life, it is a war we knew deep inside we could not possibly win!"

I proved how dumb I was by trying to be smart. "The war is over, old man, and the battle is won."

He snapped back, "Then why do you keep fighting?" "What do you mean?"

"Give it up, Youngblood; it ain't worth it."

"I am going to be somebody one day; you just wait and see. I'm going to be just like Fly Charles."

As old Bill walked away, he said, "You're going out next week, but I'll see you when you get back, if I don't read your name in the obituary column."

I would never see him again after I left, but he prophesied my future that day. Three out of every four prisoners who leave will return and they'll return having committed more serious crimes with longer sentences. For the time being, I forgot about old man Bill's lecture. I still wanted to be like Fly Charles and no one could change my mind.

Finally, the day arrived for me to depart. I had served my year, but I had not once given thought as to what direction my life should go other than the direction I had traveled in the past. I had learned to be slicker, talk smoother, be a better criminal, and get to hell much faster.

Now they were sending me back to my Promised Land more of a criminal and more of a menace, and there was nothing I could do about it. Prisons don't correct nor rehabilitate; too often, they make one worse. It was a mistake to leave this way, and some day someone would pay, someone would cry, and someone would die.

8

Going Nowhere Fast

I WAS GLAD AND rejoicing to be back in the Promised Land, but for many days I just couldn't erase the vision of Old Bill's face from my memory. Coming back to the Promised Land, I felt like a combat soldier returning to the front line; nevertheless, it was good to be home.

Certainly I thought time would have surely stood still for me, but everything had changed; and perhaps, so had I. The youngsters had gotten older, young girls had lost their virginity and were having babies, hustlers had gotten slicker, and the world events had become more violent, explosive, and maddening. But this was home and after being away for a year, I was happy to be back into the city.

My mother, sister and brothers were glad and excited to have me back home; the prodigal son had finally returned. I promised them I would straighten up. I promised to stay out of trouble, and I promised they would never have to visit me in jail or prison again—promises that I knew at the moment I had no intention to keep.

We think we know so much when we are young. We think we know all the answers to the questions and our parents know absolutely nothing. They never had to experience the pains of growing up.

What did they really know about sex, good times, and rock & roll? They were our parents and they were not supposed to know about the world in which we lived. This is what we told ourselves and forced ourselves to believe.

How many times did they tell us, "A hard head will make a soft behind." But all parental advice went into one ear and out of the other, but in the end, it was our loss. I was not aware of the fact that whenever I did something crazy or stupid that resulted in me suffering, they also felt my pains and aches. I was young, blind, ignorant, and thought I was only hurting myself. So after lying around the house for days telling lies, I heard the streets call my name, and I went running like a blind fool rushing toward my doom.

Back on the street I was introduced to the confidence game and made a living playing a short con called the Murphy. I learned the philosophy of the game and how to be a good player. I saw that the world by nature was greedy and a prime candidate for the con. Millions of people spent hours each day looking to get rich quick or searching to find a cheap bargain. They were persuaded and influenced not by reason or logic, but sound effect. No matter how ridiculous a scheme may appear, if you are able to make the scheme sound and look good, any con can be effective. This really inflated my ego because I was playing a game that was primarily reserved for much older men.

My brother was now committing violent crimes. I made an attempt to convince him the risks he were taking would always be greater than the rewards, and it would cost him more than it was worth. But who was I to tell him about right and wrong when he thought he was traveling in my step? He was attracted to crimes of violence and violence would soon claim his brief life on earth.

For the time being, I considered these the good days, and I lived like there was no tomorrow. I had taken a script playing a part in a play that had been written, produced, and designed especially for youngsters such as me. I was ignorant to the fact that the deck was stacked against me and I had no chance to win. Therefore, my destiny was already sealed.

I recalled the words of Captain McGee when I was at the training school. He once told me I wasn't a bad kid. He said I was only playing a game because I was afraid to be myself; maybe he was right after all. Who was I, and what was the real Cheese really like? For the time being, I had a date to keep with destiny and it wouldn't wait. I had a red hot date with doom and it was calling my name. I was running toward total destruction, and I was running to get there fast.

It was 1965 and I had become addicted to the streets and its way of life. I was bewitched by its charm, fascinated by its glitter, and captivated by its glamour. I was like a small coin being pulled to the very bowels of the earth by a small magnet, but I was so intoxicated with the wine of youth and the thrills of the night life, that I thought this was all of life and the way it was supposed to be lived and enjoyed. I only had one life to live, but I was living it as if it was a practice run.

1965 was also the year that Fly Charles came home, and we painted the early night with laughter and the late night with a song. Things were beginning to happen in the inner city that would change our lives and the lives of our children forever. I noticed Fly began to power his nose with coke, but he kept it under control for a while. It was good to have him back. It was as if we needed him to really make things happen for all of us.

Fly never could stay in one location too long, and after several months he went back to Chicago with his girls. It was a sad day for me when he left. We warmly embraced, and I kissed his girls goodbye and promised to see them all later in the year. But I never got the chance to see him again. I heard he went con-crazy. He could no longer tell the truth from a lie. Snorting raw coke had him seeing shadows and hearing voices that didn't exist. He had trouble trying to make a buck and the girls who had once been so loyal to him now deserted him and left him broke and all alone. And I remembered what he had once told me, "Cheese, they are always looking for greener pastures."

When I first heard the news, I was miserable and despondent for days. My mentor, the great one, that dazzling brilliant star, had fallen to the earth never to rise again. He died a flat-foot hustler, broke, unhappy, and all alone.

We all heard the unfortunate tragedy of my friend, but we learned nothing. We told ourselves we would have a storybook ending when it came our turn to be placed into the cold bosom of the earth. We said what had happened to him could never happen to us, yet none of us was half the man he was. We continued to play our games as if nothing had happened, but by the lifestyles we lived, our number could be called at any moment.

How sad it was that we learned nothing from his life and death. We continued to pattern our lives after the few men who possessed the characteristics of the Fly Charles of our world. They were the role models we strived to become; they had already arrived and we were still trying to become. What else could we do? It was useless to attempt to reach for the stars. We were black and occupied the lowest position on the social economic ladder. We were uneducated and had no vocational skills or training. We were trapped, a nation of youth disenfranchised and not permitted to be a part of America, and we were fast becoming what they said we were already, useless and no good.

This was a period in our lives that we should have mourned, but we drank champagne wine celebrating the death of a nation of black youngsters who would never reach their full potentials because they patterned their lives after ghetto hustlers who had the women, the flashy cars and clothes, and an unlimited amount of resource. If we had only known the price they paid to achieve a moment of ghetto fame, we would have flown from them in terror. If we had seen the complete picture, we would have re-entered school, sought vocational skills, and pursued a much simpler way of life.

Drugs were gradually creeping into the inner city in massive quantities, but were confined to a particular area.

Drugs in the '60s were unpopular and carried a bad stigma. For example, certain clubs wouldn't hire musicians or entertainers if they had a reputation of using heavy drugs; they were considered a bad risk and not dependable. Even hustlers used caution and were suspicious of their peers with drug habits; it was said they were not reliable or trustworthy. Because it was confined to certain areas of the inner city, if you didn't know the things to look for, you could easily miss it. And when it came to the users and abusers, they followed that age old adage, "Birds of a feather will gather together." Besides, no one was really concerned about black folks using drugs in the ghetto at that time. As long as it was confined to the inner city and away from white kids, the general concept was, "If the niggers want to kill themselves, they can go right ahead."

My little brother was still on the loose. He never confined himself to any particular area of the city; you could never pin him down. I heard he was responsible for committing robberies all over the city. Our styles were so unlike, only a few people at the time realized we were brothers. Rarely did we break the law together. It was his philosophy that one of us had to be home with mom and sis and our younger brother. But my reason was totally different from his. I just couldn't be as reckless, rash, and hotheaded as my little brother.

My lifestyle was becoming too expensive to keep up. Money became harder to hold; the more I made the more I spent. One night I committed a robbery of a food plaza with four other friends, but within two days I was broke again. I forgot about the robbery and my friends but what I didn't know was that I would definitely see them again.

I met my sister's boyfriend, and we became close friends. His name was Charles; everyone called him Chester, but I called him Chest. He was a former member of the Clovers; they were a popular recording group of the '50s and '60s. His career was temporarily put on hold because of the military; however, when he was discharged from the service, his two closest friends formed a group called the Dippers. When they became local stars, they changed their names to the Naturals and recorded several local hits for Shout Recording Label. Whenever they were performing in town, I would always go to see them. The three were extremely talented, and they had a band that was equally talented.

On my sister's twenty-third birthday, they gave her a party at the popular Colt Lounge. This was the same club in which James Whitmore shot scenes from the motion picture *Black Like Me*.

The club was crowded as usual. Although we arrived early, the club was in full swing. They had adjoining tables in a long line with alcoholic beverages of your choice. The group had to perform three shows, and when they were not on stage, they were at the table having fun. Daisy introduced me to many people who came over to wish her a happy birthday. The girls were beautiful and attractive, but none really caught my attention.

My eyes were glued to the dance floor to one girl in particular. She was a slender, dark complexioned girl who was stepping, twirling, and twisting, giving a new name to the word dancing. She danced with a great deal of feeling and passion; she stirred emotions that completely overwhelmed me. She was an artist creating magic with every move. I was in a hypnotic trance and fascinated by her charm. All the time she danced she was smiling. And when the music stopped, she didn't walk off the floor, she gracefully strolled with an air of complete confidence. She was the best, and she knew it. My eyes accompanied her to a nearby table where she joined two other girls. WOW! I thought; she could be the prize I have lived all my life to win.

I momentarily forgot her, and I was engaged in a busy conversation with Daisy and Chester when I heard the sound of a perfect pitch.

"Hi Daisy."

I was astonished; it was the prize, and she was still smiling. "Hi Jean," my sister said.

"I didn't know today was your birthday," she said, taking a seat directly across from me.

I was trying to act unconcerned and ignored her, but I wasn't doing such of a good job. Every few seconds our eyes met and locked. Her eyes were large with black pupils, and she continued to smile with an occasional burst of laughter.

Daisy noticed our stare. "Jean," she said, "this is my big brother Cheese."

I looked into her eyes and heard exhilarating music playing on the cords of my soul. Our spirits seemed to reach out and touch for a moment that night. The band was playing a very slow song. I reached across the table and asked, "Would you like to dance?" She placed her small gentle hand in mine, and I led her toward the dance floor. And that was the beginning of our relationship.

She was a lot of fun and easy to talk to. She was only seventeen and lived in Northeast. She had two sisters and was a professional dancer. I also found out that night, although it was common knowledge, she was considered the best dancer in town. Before the night was over, she gave me her address and phone number, and I promised her I would call the following night. But it would be years before I had the opportunity to keep that promise, but keep it I would.

I was still rambling, still searching, and still trying to find my niche in the world. I knew I belonged somewhere in the world, but where? I was still running in the race I had entered so long ago, and I was determined to get there faster than anyone else. Every now and then I'd pause and turn around, but all I saw was pain and anguish, and when I looked toward the finish line, all I saw was the grave.

"RUN! RUN faster!" I heard imaginary voices shouting in my ear, so I kept on running—to cross the finish line. What would the prize for the winner be? Who would be there to cheer me as I crossed my finish line? Would there be an audience of jubilant fans applauding as they raised my hand the victor?

It didn't matter how I won; all that really mattered was that I win. All that mattered was for me to cross the line before anyone else. How long had I been running? How much ground had I already covered, and how much distance could there be left? I continued to run with breakneck speed toward my finish line.

One night while I was out scanning an area near New Hampshire Avenue I heard someone call my name.

"Cheese?"

Immediately I turned around without thinking and answered, "Yea." But I didn't like what I saw. Yards away stood two men dressed in blue jeans. Instantly I recognized that they were the police. They had caught me off guard. They were sure if they called me by my real name they would have alerted me, but calling me by my nickname, instantly I would respond. And they had guessed right.

"We have a warrant for your arrest," one of them said.

"A warrant for my arrest; for what?"

"Someone is interested in talking to you about a robbery."

At first I panicked, but then I told myself it was just one of those mistakes the police make everyday, but it wasn't. I was taken into custody and charged with the food plaza robbery.

What would it take for me to realize that crime really doesn't pay if you're black and poor? What would it take for me to understand I was fighting a losing battle? How could I possibly win when everyone held a royal straight flush and I was bluffing with a lousy pair of deuces? Again, black folk should run from crime, but I ran full speed toward it.

I was ushered before a magistrate; bail was set and a date for a preliminary hearing, and back to the district jail I went. Because of the seriousness of my charge, I was assigned to cell block two.

As I entered the cell block an older con was sitting behind a desk answering the phone and filling out papers. Over the desk was a large board with cell numbers and inmates who occupied them. The con who sat behind the desk was in charge of the block and those who worked sanitation and served the food during meals had privileges other cons didn't have. They were allowed much more freedom of movement and their cell doors were open most of the time.

The convict behind the desk pointed to the board and asked, "Is there any particular cell you'd like to go in?"

I must have stood looking the board over too long. "Well, what's it going to be, Youngblood?"

"My name ain't Youngblood, and it doesn11 matter where you put me." I knew that I was in the doghouse, and if you wanted to survive you had to act like a dog in most cases. If you displayed any sign of weakness, the dogs ate you alive. Still there was no classification system. As before, if your bond was more than a thousand dollars, everyone was mixed in together, and age was not a factor.

Here I met old friends from the training school and others whom I didn't know. But we all had three things in common; we were all black, all poor, and all had a story.

"I was innocent. I was framed." We all had our stories to tell.

"I was at home with my lady when those dudes robbed that bank. But I'm black, poor, uneducated, and have a criminal record, so I took a cop and pleaded guilty. What else could I do?"

"I didn't get any justice in the courtroom; justice is blind in one eye and sees what it wants to see. What other reason would the statute wear a blindfold?"

"My folks are trying to raise money for my appeal so that I can beat this bum-rap, and you can bet when I do, I am going to sue for defamation of character."

We all had our stories to tell, but as I listened to many of these stories I was totally convinced that many of them were indeed innocent of the crimes they allegedly committed. Seventy to ninety percent of these men had pleaded guilty as the result of a plea bargain, and not necessarily because of guilt. They had a guilt; they were born with a guilt of being born black, poor, and a member of the underclass. So I sat and listened to stories where the innocent pleaded GUILTY!

One glimpse inside any jail in America and you will see that equality under the law does not exist. You can easily observe that the legal system worked almost exclusively against the poor man, and rarely will you see the extremely wealthy and middle-class prosecuted as defendants. For example, ten executives of a major corporation were convicted in 1961 for price-fixing involving tens of millions of dollars, but they only spent months in prison. But still, society did not consider them to be criminals.

On the other hand, if a black youth is charged with stealing a few dollars from a grocery store, not only was he considered a criminal by society, but if an officer shot him down in the street, nine times out of ten, it would be ruled justifiable homicide. So equality under the law was, in fact, a myth.

It is a general assumption that everyone who is in jail is guilty of committing a crime, but a second glimpse inside any jail in America and you'll see that this is not the case at all. First of all, only a number of law violations are reported and detected, so there are more law breakers in society than jails. Secondly, over half of all people in jails have not been convicted of any crimes; they spend months and even years awaiting trial. Finally, as mentioned several times earlier, seventy to ninety percent plead guilty without a trial because they cannot afford an attorney, don't trust a public defender, and would appear guilty when they are actually innocent.

Yes, we all had our stories to tell. But it was a fact that black kids from the ghetto who had their first encounter with the law were branded with a criminal record that would never happen if they were white or middle class. Although I was guilty, I could really relate to these stories, because I too was a member of the underclass and felt the unevenness and inequality of the system.

Every Friday afternoon on the fifth tier they had Muslim service. I first started going to get out of the cell, but then I got interested. They did not have to teach me to hate; I was already full of it. I sat on the edge of the steel bench listening to a religious doctrine that kept me coming back for more. William T. X. Fulwood was the assigned minister, and later he recruited me and made me his assistant minister. He gave me a stack of papers consisting of lessons and laws I had to learn. When I was locked in my cell, Brother Fulwood stayed at my door telling me about our leader the Elijah Muhammad and the early followers of the movement. I was so caught up in the movement I completely forgot about my case. Brother Fulwood was a very articulate speaker and had the ability to attract and hold any audience. The highlight of my week was Friday at 1 p.m.

Brother Fulwood stood behind the podium with his bald head gleaming and perspiration running from his forehead teaching about the crimes committed against black folks.

"For too long," he screamed, "we've sat and witnessed the atrocities committed against us simply because the color of our skin happened to be black. For too long we've seen white folks kill in the name of mercy, murder in the name of peace, and destroy in the name of love."

Vividly, we saw large veins criss-crossing his forehead and bulging from his large neck. For forty-five minutes, words flew from his mouth like bullets from a machine gun.

"The two greatest evils the world has ever known are committed in the name of God and love."

After weeks of instructions and coaching, I was officially made his assistant. Now on most Fridays I stood behind the rostrum teaching against a system that had been founded on slavery and injustice. Some of my friends were now calling me a fanatic. They said if I spent as much time studying my case I could walk away a winner. But they were fools I told myself; didn't these simple fools know this was the dawn of a new day!

The Moslem and Muslim religions have always attracted large followers in jails and prisons. Malcolm's words, "If you kill my dog, you better hide your cat," was our kind of talk, the language we understood best. All our lives we were told nothing and made to feel ashamed because we were black, but now we were told that we were actually better than white folks, and were superior not inferior. For instance, the black man had a rich and wealthy civilization when they were roaming the hills and caves of Europe living like beasts. Although we were poor, we were made to feel like we were somebody. These religions caught our attention because they were religions for warriors, and were we all not warriors? They also caught the younger brothers' attention because it was a shelter from the bandits who looked for young victims to use like girls.

By this time I had gone overboard and didn't realize it. Every time I heard the word Christian I would go into a rage; I took every opportunity to verbally and physically persecute them.

When my trial came, I pleaded not guilty because I was sure the government couldn't prove me guilty beyond a reasonable doubt. I had one co-defendant on this charge; the other two were not apprehended. We had a long trial and a crowded courtroom. Our trial lasted five days and the jury deliberated two days.

The government had twelve witnesses, and all twelve eyewitnesses took the stand and testified for the government. All twelve positively identified my co-defendant as one of the four bandits that night. But only one of the twelve could identify me. She was a young white female in her 20s.

I'll never forget when she was sworn in and took the stand.

"Do you see the man or men in this courtroom that you recognize as one of the armed men on the night in question?" the district attorney asked.

"Yes I do."

"Would you please identify the man or men for the court."

The witness did not hesitate to point to my co-defendant and slowly she pointed to me also. The district attorney didn't worry about my co-defendant, he had him and he knew it. Now, he focused his attention on me.

"Now this man, how can you identify him?" He pointed to me waiting for a reply.

"I can identify him by his large brown eyes."

When I heard her answer, I almost fell out of my chair. If that was all they had, I was sure to walk on this one. There was no way the government could get a conviction and find me guilty on her testimony.

The D. A. had made a mistake and attempted to correct it. "Are you sure," still pointing at me, "this is one of the men who robbed the food plaza the night in question?"

She had been one of the cashiers. "I am absolutely sure he is one of the men; I'll never forget his eyes."

Now, my attorney had one task; of the twelve witnesses who took the stand, she was the only one who could identify me. His job was simple, destroy her testimony.

On cross examination he questioned the witness. "Let me be sure that I understand you correctly. Are you identifying my client only by his eyes?" He didn't give her an opportunity to respond. He continued his cross examination.

"Not his height, not his complexion, only his eyes!" He took a brief pause. "Did you notice any scars, marks, or any other outstanding feature about my client?"

"No, his eyes are the only thing I remember," she managed to say in a low voice.

"Oh yes!" my attorney snapped, "his eyes."

I tried to see if we were winning any ground with the jury but it was difficult to tell.

"If I saw Mr. Cheese for the first time," my lawyer went on, "I would remember his height, maybe his hair, his complexion, and then maybe—his eyes."

"All that I know", she said, "I will never forget his eyes; they were large, brown, and glassy."

"Your place of business is located primarily in a black neighborhood, and most of your patrons are black; are they not?"

"Yes, they are."

"You stand on your feet for eight hours a day, and you see hundreds of customers during the course of that day. Yet, am I to believe you can identify my client only by his eyes, seeing him for the first time in a matter of minutes?"

He looked at the jury in disbelief; then to my amazement, he sprang a surprise. He called the name of a spectator in the courtroom, "Would you take a good look at this gentleman?" After she observed him carefully, he asked,

"Do you recognize him; have you ever seen him before?"

"No, I haven't," she replied with an air of confidence.

"I find that rather strange," he said. "This gentleman came into your establishment, purchased items, got into your checkout line, and was waited on by you? He even had a casual conversation with you, and this was less than 36 hours ago, and you can't identify him? Then how in the world can you positively identify my client 30 odd days later after seeing him only for a few minutes?"

He turned to the jury and said with a look of disdain, "I have no further questions, your Honor."

What a performance. I looked at my sister who was in the courtroom with a smile of victory. I was certain I had won. There was no possible way the government could get a guilty verdict from the jury on that testimony, and I knew that I was going home.

After two days of deliberation, the jury returned with a verdict. They had found my co-defendant guilty on all counts. I was mentally sitting there preparing to walk out the courtroom, but I thought I heard the foreman say the word guilty behind my name. I was so preoccupied I hadn't heard them say the word "not" in front of guilty.

Then I got the shock of my life. I didn't hear the word "not" because he hadn't said it, but he did say guilty, and the judge confirmed it. The jury had found us both guilty of armed robbery.

I was the reason the jury deliberated so long. They couldn't place me in the food plaza that night, but they could place me with my co-defendant. His own parents had said I was with him shortly after the robbery. If they had found me not guilty, they would have to find him not guilty also.

When we went back for sentencing, he received nine years and I received six. My trial was never a question of me being guilty. The evidence presented said otherwise. After this experience, I was convinced if you are black and charged with a crime, it is automatically assumed that you are guilty. I stayed in jail less than a month and was transferred to the Lorton Youth Center.

The Youth Center was built in the '60s for youthful offenders 18 to 24 years old who had been sentenced under the youth correctional act. Compared to the other institutions I had been in, it wasn't bad at all. It had a small population and only four dorms. It had the appearance of a small college campus instead of an institution.

Each dorm had four wings with approximately 20 rooms each, and every inmate had his own key and private room. They had an excellent vocational and academic school. Here you had the opportunity to get an education or learn a skill trade. I told

Each Night, I Die

myself I was too smart to get in school, so I chose to work in the carpenter shop. Everything was there if you wanted to take the advantage of it. Everything was within your reach, and all you had to do was reach out. But something was still wrong, not with the institution, but with me. I didn't have the desire to reach out and I didn't understand why. Why did I continue to play games and think that wrong was right, more was better, and everything that glittered was gold? Everything was there for us to turn it around, but only a few did.

The Youth Center was best known for its boxing team; that was its trademark. They had a legendary boxing team and it was here that I learned to box. They had Golden Gloves Champs, National AAU Champions, and produced some ranked professionals.

When you refuse to do right, you choose to do wrong; and that is what we did. We walked the compound until 11 p.m., listening to sweet sounds of WHUR, and thinking about ways to come back to prison.

So many things happened in my life in such a short time. My brother was finally convicted and sent to training school. Cindy who was such a sweet young girl had died from a drug overdose. Daisy and Chest had two boys and made me an uncle twice, and finally my parole date was getting near. When I did go up, to my surprise, the parole board granted me parole.

All my life I had been caught up playing games that I couldn't win, yet I continued to play. Why couldn't I stop and do the right thing instead of the wrong? I had gone too far, I told myself, and I couldn't turn back now. I had paid my fee to enter the race, and I was still determined to cross the finish line.

As my release date got closer, the nights got longer. One day I was in my room reading an Ebony magazine when an interesting article caught my attention; it was a story on Washington's best go-go dancers. This style of dancing had just arrived on the scene and had everyone's attention. The story had several of the best dancers in the city. At first glance, one of the faces looked familiar. I looked closer and it hit me like a ton of bricks. It was Jean, my prize; that was why her face looked so familiar. She looked different; maybe it was because I had never seen her picture in a magazine before. But it was her all right. She had given me her number, but I was so busy running, I didn't have time to pick up the phone and call her.

I sat there staring at her picture with my mouth hanging open. I sat there for what seemed like hours. What was it about her? Just her picture filled my head with thoughts of her that seemed to carry me off to a paradise where life was sweet and my world for a moment was a beautiful dream. I knew I had to see her again, and I had to see her before I crossed the finish line.

It was 1967 and I was going back home—home to a place that would always hold it against me, not because of what I was, but because of where I had been.

9

Too Far To Turn Back

"He who starts behind in the race of life must forever remain behind or he must run faster than the one who is ahead."

Dr. Benjamin Mays

I WAS 24 AND leaving prison again. I was still living a dream, a dream that was locked inside my head and I lived it every day of my life. I was still running like a hound dog was snapping at my heel; I was chasing a dream like a June bug chased a scent in the summer sun. Look at me world, I cried! Stop me, please! But I had gone too far and run too long to turn back now. It seemed as if death lay around every corner, but I couldn't stop nor turn back simply because I had gone too far.

They said I could never be anything other than what I already was, a convict and criminal. There wasn't a ghost of a chance of me ever rising from the slums and ghetto to become a physician or an architect. I couldn't even get a job that paid minimum wages because they said I was street poisoned and had gone too far to turn back. This is what they said; this is what I also thought; and this is how I lived. In most instances, what you think will determine how you act.

I still had a date with destiny. I still had a dream and a finish line to cross. But at times I felt like an old man rocking in a chair; I had movement, but I wasn't going anywhere, and the closer I got to the finish line, the farther it moved away. But my dream was real, and the elusive finish line was a constant picture before my face.

I wish I could say it was about necessities, or perhaps force; but it wasn't. It was all about choices. This was the life I had chosen. This was my dream and my life, and no one could live it or run it but me.

When I was released from the Youth Center, I had to go to a halfway house because I was in parole. The halfway house that I went to was located on the corner of 13th and T streets Northwest. It was next door to the Whitelaw Hotel that was also one of the biggest drug dens and shooting galleries in the city. The halfway house was also just one short block from the legendary 14th and T, one of the major drug corners in all of Washington. I could never understand the logic of them having a halfway house in the center of this drug infested area. Was it to test our strength? Was it to test our will? I am sure they had a logical reason, but I am not sure it was wise. Many couldn't wait to walk that one short block to find out who had the best drugs on the market.

When I reported to my parole officer, I was surprised; it was Mr. Wilson, one of the officers from the training school. Since my adjustment was just about perfect in the house, they released me; and I went home—home to the streets, and it never looked so good.

14th and T was like a beautiful voluptuous woman all aglow. She held out her outstretched arms and I embraced her like a long lost lover. She whispered enticing words into my ears and convinced me that I was still the star of her show. But in reality, she was a promiscuous tramp with funky underarms and dirty pants.

Washington was being invaded with a fresh new style. Professional gentlemen of leisure from various northern and southern states set up temporary shop in grand style. The confidence men were more flamboyant. The girls were more seductive and aggressive. Everyone was doing his own individual thing, and this was considered by most as the apex era of hustling.

Each Night, I Die

Drugs had slowly emerged from the cracks and corners of the inner city. Customers and consumers came in huge numbers from surrounding metropolitan communities to purchase these drugs. The ruling class was much too intelligent to allow such a dangerous enemy to live within its mist. So they came into our communities from all over to buy a deadly white powder that guaranteed to solve all their immediate problems, cure all their pains, and make the weight they carried on their shoulders suddenly seem as light as a feather. They came in droves to buy this magic powder in a small capsule for a dollar and a half that would cure all their past, present, and future ills.

They also came after dark, in all kinds of weather, to warm their cold frustrated souls for the standard price of ten and two. They came because they also lived in a world of plastic and artificial dreams that were not, could not, ever be real. And me, where did I fit in? I came because I loved the streets, and I had gone too far to turn around; and I came because this was home.

1967 was a tragic year for me; it was the year that I became addicted to heroin. One night I ran into an old friend from my training school and youth center days; his name was Kenny. I had only been with him a short time when his conversation turned toward drugs. I think he assumed that I was already trapped like him as so many of our friends were with drugs. As he talked I looked around and observed the scene. Standing a few feet away was a friend that we both knew from the school, Phillip. He began shooting heroin shortly after his release in 1961, and now he was a dope-fiend.

The best Phillip could do now was to try to play a nickel and dime short con and commit petty thievery to support his habit. He stood in the middle of the busy sidewalk with both knees bent in a sitting position. His head was arched toward the pavement, and his eyes were closed as if he was in a deep trance. At regular intervals his right hand moved from his side to his forehead; it made two or three slow motion movements along his face, and then dropped back to his side. His mouth hung wide open, and he made several attempts to stand upright, but he never made it.

Farther up the street was a girl named Brenda; she had once been a gorgeous girl, but now all that was evident of her beauty was perhaps her figure. Although she was still young in years, turning two bit tricks and shooting high grade heroin had made her old and ugly long before her time.

I looked and I became curious; a drug that could be this powerful had to be good. Oh, I should have turned and ran as fast and as far as I could, but I didn't. Instead, I was ready to try it for the first time. I was more than a fool rushing in where wise men never tread. I've made many mistakes in my life, but none as big and costly as this.

I'll never forget that night; I sold my very soul for a moment of pleasure; but I had no idea what it would take to redeem it, or how long. I felt the rush, and my head exploded into what seemed like a thousand pieces. My mouth became dry, and my head began to spin; my vision was losing its focus, and everything was moving in slow motion. Small beads of perspiration formed on my forehead, and I tried to speak, but my voice was suddenly hoarse.

Now I understood how a powerful white horse could mount your back and ride you straight to hell. It had complete control over me; it was like I had no will of my own. I sat there drifting off with a false sense of confidence. I felt like I was the greatest man that ever walked the earth. I could accomplish any deed and perform any task; I was a slave completely under its control.

They said this was considered the apex era for hustlers; if that was true, it was also a period of mourning for those who struggled for progress and a larger piece of the American pie. They struggled to free themselves from the evil hand of oppression and racism while we struggled to remain in slavery.

We were guilty as charged of glamorizing a lifestyle that perpetrated an evil and oppressive system that kept us in total darkness and slavery. We tried to defend and intellectualize our conduct as being rational, but it only proved that our ignorance was without measure. Who among us could truthfully argue this style we had freely adopted was not a form of modem slavery? Oh yes! This was indeed the era of the '60s, the so-called apex for street hustlers, but for those who struggle to get ahead, we were a curse, and we set them back a hundred years. They fought to cast off the mental chains of slavery, but we demanded by our actions and deeds that the chains remain intact.

At the time, I honestly thought I was making ground moving forward toward the finish line, but every step I advanced forward I also took three backward. Black leaders were beginning to mount the speaker's platform speaking about black consciousness and race pride, yet we fought to remain slaves by choice, not by force. The more these leaders talked about freedom the farther we moved away; we had eyes to see, but we were blind; we had ears to hear, but were deaf.

Drugs—wasn't this another form of slavery? Drugs became a part of our culture, and they complemented each other like a hand in a glove. But was not this a way that the so-called master race practiced systematic genocide on the "have nots"? Oh no! They did not hold a gun to our heads and force us to use drugs; they were too smart for that. They just created a condition of hopelessness and despair that made us willing slaves by choice. We took a bite from the forbidden fruit that dangled before our eyes and sat in a stupor as the whole world and life passed us by.

We just wanted to try it one time; we could handle it; this is what we told ourselves. But that too was a lie. Just one time was all we wanted, but in the end once wasn't quite enough, but two was far too many. We neglected our health; we abandoned our families, and drugs became the mistress we loved and the god we served. Nat Turner, Sojourner Truth, Harriet Tubman, and William Lloyd Garrison all sacrificed their lives for the freedom and better life for our people, but we freely surrendered our will to drugs and a lifestyle that made us enemies of the very heroes that fought to set us free.

Benjamin Mays had said, "He who starts behind in the race of life must forever remain behind or he must run faster than the one who is ahead." Wasn't it enough that we had entered the race at a disadvantage and miles behind; then, why did we fight so hard to perpetuate a way of life that caused us nothing but suffering, slavery, and an early death? No force was needed now because we surrendered without a struggle, without a fight, and without a conflict.

We were so caught up in our own destruction that we couldn't hear what the other side was saying, nor did we care. We continued to surrender time and time again to the pleasures of life for an instant, but the day after they made us weep in pain; it was instant pleasure, but endless pain, as if life didn't come with enough pain already. It didn't have to be this way; it shouldn't have been this way, but this was the way it was.

One night my friend Nick and I were driving down Florida Avenue when two girls caught my attention. They were almost at the intersection of Rhode Island Avenue, walking east when we slowly passed them. They were both wearing full-length black leather coats. Wait a minute! That walk, what was it about that walk? Frantically I searched my memory to recall what it was, and why I was suddenly so excited. It wasn't a walk but a stroll, and I was sure I had seen it somewhere before...

Instantly I recognized her even before she turned around. How could I forget it? It was her! One of the girls approaching the car was Jean. My mind went back to the night I met her at my sister's birthday party, and recently when I saw her picture in the magazine. Now here she was again walking into my life like a beautiful vision that appeared at least once in a sleeper's dream. Here she was again, the girl I had to have before I crossed my finish line. This time there would be no getting away, and she didn't.

In many ways we were alike. She would pay a price to see her name in lights, and I would pay any price to reach the finish line and see the Promised Land. I will never forget the very first time that I held her in my arms and felt the warmth and heat from her tender body; I knew then that I would pay any price to make her mine. Holding her I went temporarily insane. There was something about her that made me want her more than anything else. Holding her meant more than the dream I lived, more than the finish line, and more than life itself. All the things I could achieve and accomplish in life would mean absolutely nothing without her. It was as if she had cast a spell on me from which I would never be totally free.

Soon we moved in together and made plans to be married. We promised to love each other for a lifetime. We promised that the dawn of each new day would find us tightly embraced in each other's arms. But we were in love and surely we didn't know that the way we felt today was no guarantee that we would feel the same tomorrow. The whole world changes; we change, and nothing remains the same. So how could I promise to love her for a lifetime? How could I try to possess her love? When in truth, I didn't even possess myself. I thought about my loving parents when they were young. Hadn't they also made the same promises? How many miles would we walk together? Would our lives be full of tears and heartaches? What would life really have in store for us? Only time would tell.

Many years later I would read a poem in a lonely prison cell, and thoughts of her would flood my mind.

> *"There will be new dreams,*
> *Replacing those that fell apart,*
> *For life is never what it seems.*
> *There will be new hope To mend a child's broken heart,*
> *For love is made of broken dreams."*
>
> *Anonymous*

How was I to know what would become of us? And will I ever be able to read, without weeping, the final chapter of our story? That would be many years to come, but for the time being our lives had only begun.

The Dippers had changed their name to the Naturals. They had signed a contract with Shout and had a hit record on the chart. It seemed like every time you turned on the radio some station was playing their song, "Lickin Stick." They were constantly on the road traveling. One week they would be at the Apollo in New York;

the next week they would be doing a live television show in Philly. They were in demand because they had a record on the charts.

Chest and I were like brothers. In fact he called me brother-in-law; consequently, the rest of the group and friends called me the same. Many times Daisy made the remark, "The two of you should have been brothers; you are so much alike." I think it broke his heart when he found out I was using heroin.

I was standing in a popular all night carry-out on 14th Street, it was past 3 a.m., and so crowded you could hardly enter. Early morning customers on their way home came in and placed orders and quickly left. Working girls came in from the cold to avoid the chilly wind. Gamblers came in from nearby night spots to take a break from the crap tables and get a bite to eat. Drug dealers came in to be sure no one had to go in without their wake-up shot, and hustlers dropped in to be sure they had taken care of all their business for the night.

I was standing among this sea of humanity when he entered and made his way toward me.

"Hey brother-in-law," he said with that usual wide smile on his face, "are you going in any time soon?"

"I'll be by later," I told him; I was in a world all of my own.

I noticed his stare and wondered why, but I didn't have to wonder long.

"Man, brother-in-law, have you been oiling?"

I think he already knew the answer; he had seen the look too many times before, but I knew somehow he was hoping he was wrong. But he wasn't. He was one of the first in my family to know that I was using drugs.

"I only use it now and then, Chest. I can handle it."

But his pain only intensified. "You got to stop, man, before it is too late. Mainlining is for losers. Nobody can handle that stuff like that. Please man, you got to stop before it's too late."

I must have been seeing or imagining things; he looked at me in a way I'll never forget. Why were his eyes suddenly misty? They couldn't be tears because no friend had ever cried for me. He put his

Each Night, I Die

arms around my shoulder, and we walked out into the cool morning air. Soon the sun would rise, and we would all disappear back into our holes until the following night, leaving the streets to those who made an honest and legitimate living working 9 to 5.

Somewhere from a long almost forgotten memory I recalled an old quotation from the book of Job. "Man that is born of a woman is of few days, and full of trouble."

One night I went with Daisy to a club when the group was booked for an engagement. Chest was to meet us there, but he never made it. He never missed a show nor had he ever been late. Still we waited, but no Chest. I took her home and tried to assure her that everything was all right, but deep inside, I was beginning to worry.

Later that night the phone finally rang, and she snatched it from the cradle. She listened for a few minutes and began to weep. He had been in an auto accident and was in what is now the Greater Southeast Hospital.

She rushed to him in tears and was a nervous wreck. She had to be with him. He was in intensive care and on the critical list. Daisy sat by his side around the clock. She came home to shower and change clothes and back to his bedside she went.

After a week or so, his condition improved, and he was moved out of intensive care. She came home and gave us the good news and I went back to see him with her. When I saw him, he was in good spirits; he even tried to joke and laugh with the tubes in his nose.

"Sis," I told her, "he is going to be all right."

"Thank God," was all that she could say.

I tried to spend more time with her, and my mother was always at her side. I was with her on the day the phone rang; it was a ring that would change her life forever.

I saw her pick up the phone; she held it to her ear for only a minute, and the receiver fell to the floor. I looked at her in a state of shock. Paralyzed, I watched her open her mouth wide as if she tried to scream, yet no sound escaped. She was paralyzed and unable to move, and her mouth was still wide open. Suddenly she fell to her knees as if the weight of her body was too heavy. She began to swing and fight the air with her small fist and tears ran like a flood from her eyes. She shook her head from side to side in disbelief as if what she had just heard would soon go away. When her voice returned, all I heard her say was one word.

"No! No!" Again and again she screamed.

I felt a ball of tension burning inside my chest. I tried to shut out the sight and sound of a reality that was too much for even me to bear. No one had to tell me that he was dead. Chest was gone forever; that was the meaning of it all. My nephews had lost a father; my sister had lost a loving companion, and I had lost a dear friend.

I never realized how uncertain life could be. I should have, but I didn't. Suddenly I felt like an old man, and all I wanted to do was forget. Why did life have to be this way? Why did the good have to die so young? Why did the world have to be this way?

There are many things in this life we will never be able to understand or explain. From birth to death we are forced to live with them not knowing what they mean and ignorant to their reasons. Yet somehow, we must live with them from day to day. They grow and become a part of us and become secrets that we take with us to our graves. So strange is life, we are not even permitted to know what it is all about. So we go through life screaming-WHY? Why did he have to die when he had so much to live for? Why were we preparing to place his body in an earth that would soon forget his existence? WHY?

We buried him at Lincoln Memorial Cemetery. It was February 1968, an afternoon of bright sunshine. And as I looked up at the sun, I thought, how could the sun shine so bright, and everything in my life be so cold and dark?

My brother was becoming more aggressive with each passing day. He had developed a philosophy that everything you have is mine if I am strong enough to take it. When I attempted to talk to him, it was useless; he never listened. Why should he? In reality there was no difference between the two of us. To him he also had a dream to live, and he didn't need my approval. It was his dream, and he was determined to live it, just as I was determined to live mine.

One night when I came home Jean was with her best friend Annette, and they both were acting strangely. I noticed them doing a lot of whispering.

"What are you two whispering about?" I wanted to know.

"Jean has something to tell you," Annette replied.

"But, Annette, I told you."

Annette stopped her before she could finish. "If you don't tell him, I will; but he should hear it from you. You should be the one to tell him."

"Tell me what?" I had no idea what they were talking about.

"I am pregnant," Jean said softly.

But it was loud enough for me to hear. I rushed to her with a loud scream as I lifted her in my arms. I couldn't believe it; I was going to be a father. I placed my hand on her stomach and rubbed it gently.

"We have to take care of my son."

"But how do you know it is going to be a boy?" she wanted to know.

"I am sure of it."

Approximately nine months later I was arrested and charged with the Harrison Narcotic Act (possession of heroin), and I found myself back in the DC jail. It was the same old routine and same old familiar faces.

The first day passed, and I didn't hear from Jean. The second and third day and still no word from her. On the fourth day, I was beginning to worry. A variety of negative thoughts entered my head. Had she run off and deserted me? Had she had an accident? Then why wasn't I out on bail? Why was I still here?

"Hey, Cheese," someone called from the front of the dorm, "they are calling your name for a visit."

I wasn't sure who it was, but I couldn't wait to get there. When I got there, I went to the end of the long visiting booth and sat down.

I picked up the phone and looked in the small diamond shaped window, and there she was. Her eyes sparkled like I had never seen them before.

She picked up the receiver and the words she spoke, the way she spoke them, melted my heart.

"Look! Look at our son." She pulled her chair back, and I saw him for the first time.

He was lying in her lap dressed all in blue, wrapped in a blue blanket. I was at a loss for words. He was the cutest yet largest baby I had ever seen; he weighed nine pounds and ten ounces. As I sat there looking at him in his mother's lap, I momentarily thought about my father; he wanted me to be just like him. But this was my son, and I didn't want him to be anything like me. He would be a doctor, a lawyer, or even an athlete. But he would be everything that I wasn't.

"I called from the hospital and told them to tell you I was in the hospital, but they didn't tell you. Did they?"

"No," I shook my head. "That is why I was worried about you."

"The bondsman is on his way over to get you out. Do you want me to wait for you?"

"No, take our son home. I'll be there as soon as I am released."

The guard came and let us know that our visit had expired.

As she was leaving, I tapped on the window and called her back. "What is his name?"

"It is the same as yours," she said with a beautiful smile.

I rushed back upstairs and told my friends the news; I had a son, and shortly after they called my name to be released on bond. But everything would be different this time, because now I had a son.

10

Out of Control

TIME PASSED SWIFTLY, THE days were long, and the nights were brief. It was 1970 already, and I didn't know where the time had gone. I had so much to live for, and I should've slowed down and evaluated my life, but I didn't; I couldn't. I still told myself I had a dream to live, a finish line to cross, and a Promised Land to see. The bad times were all behind me now, and only the good days lay ahead.

This is the lie that I told myself, but hadn't life taught me the calm is always before the storm? Didn't I realize the hand on the clock was slowly turning and time would soon run out for me? But when you are out of control the dark seems bright and the wrong seems right.

Finally I went to court on the old drug charge. Every time the judge set a date for trial I got a continuance. But now the day arrived and I had to stand before another judge who was to decide my future. My attorney entered a plea of not guilty. According to the law there was no probable cause for the officers to stop my car, so anything they obtained in the search was illegal. Although the trial was technical, it was over in a matter of minutes before it reached a jury.

The government took the position that the officers were performing their duty and the routine check was legal. However, when my attorney cross examined the arresting officer, he established that the arrest was illegal; they had no right to stop my automobile. The government claimed I looked suspicious on the 1900 block of Fourteenth Street, in the car with three black females on a Sunday afternoon; that was presumptuous. Also, they assumed the white powder in the capsules was heroin; however, when the judge requested the analysis report, the district attorney couldn't product it.

The judge was furious. "Am I to understand this case has been on the docket for months and no one has filed a report to analyze the suspected drugs? Then what evidence does the court have that the powder was in fact a narcotic?"

I could hardly believe it. Events didn't ordinarily occur like this in a court of law, especially when you are black and poor.

The judge continued. "Are we to assume it was heroin? This court cannot deal with assumptions; it must deal with facts. I've asked you attorneys to be prepared when you come before this court, but you continue to come unprepared, and I will not tolerate it." He looked down from his high position and announced loud and clear, "I find the defendant not guilty; case dismissed."

Who was it that had said justice was blind? It could see after all.

My son was growing larger by the day. He brought so much love and happiness into our lives, and he was extremely smart for being so small. I began to see so much of myself in him that at times it frightened me. Still, he must not be anything like his father. At times many parents are guilty of having a brainless love for their children. I love flowers, but I don't know how to care for them or how to prevent them from dying, so I have a brainless love for flowers as we at times have a brainless love for our children. How could I love him so much when I went on dreaming and trying to beat an invisible clock?

One day I ran into an old friend. He was going into the drug business and he was looking for a good partner. His name was Jo-Jo and he prided himself as being clever.

"Cheese, my man," he told me. "Drugs are the business of the future, and one day I see it as being big as IBM and AT&T. We can make a rather small investment today and make a huge profit tomorrow, and at the same time get our names established in the market..."

Although I thought he had gone a bit too far about IBM and AT&T, we did form a partnership, but it didn't last long. When drug dealers retire, it is to a prison or to a cemetery. There is no real success or future; it is pain, torment, shame, and disaster.

Years ago I had become a modem slave by choice; but now I compounded my madness by becoming a modern slave-holder as well; I sold death and destruction to all those who wished to remain a slave to me. I and countless others made a profit off the misery and suffering of our own people. I was so out of control and my heart was so hardened I was not the least bit moved by the deplorable conditions I saw.

Thieves came with valuable merchandise that was stolen from merchants to exchange for a poison substance that kept them bound in chains; they stole property from homes and property owners and brought their booty to the feet of the dealers who smiled when they saw them coming. Welfare mothers also came; they were trapped in a life of deprivation and guilt, seeking physical relief from the pains of living; so they sacrificed all their tomorrows for a moment of brief pleasure. Legitimate citizens came who had once been outspoken against the drug epidemic; now their voices were silent because that would quickly transform them from the have to the have-nots, and from the legitimate to the unlawful.

I was fully conscious of this horrible state and appalling conditions, yet I was a co-conspirator used in the plot to practice genocide against my own people. LOOK—this is what I did to my own. I was a co-conspirator used in the vicious plot to systematically destroy my own people, and I was totally out of control. Look at the sins that I and countless others committed in the name of greed and profit. For one dollar we could get ahead, for one dollar we could be admired, and for one dollar we could smell the scent of burning flesh and not be moved by the smell. We became the enemies of our people, and we became the enemies of ourselves. There is an enemy that lives deep within, that I've hated all my life. I've hated this enemy because it is evil, cruel, and deceitful. For years I've seen shades and silhouettes of its image, but today it has been named and identified. Today it can no longer remain nameless and anonymous; at last its deceit must be exposed.

I asked my enemy, "Why do you hate me; why do you oppress me and keep me ignorant, uneducated, and poor?" But it remains speechless as if I was the evil one.

It was then that I realized in order for me to live, I must slay it, and the enemy must die. The two of us could no longer exist; one must live, and the other must die.

Face to face we stood. I pulled my weapon to strike the final blow, but as I was delivering the crushing blow, my hand became suspended in mid-air. The enemy's face became crystal clear, and the enemy was myself! Today I met the enemy for the very first time, but to kill the enemy is to also kill myself. How can I kill myself? How can I kill the beast within? One day, I would have to kill it or it would continue to kill me.

On my trips to New York I would see Edna; she was still young and beautiful. It was like time had stood still for her because she hadn't aged at all. Although time had stood still, we certainly had changed. The flame I once carried for her had diminished to a flicker, and neither of us had the desire to attempt to call back yesterday. But we would always remain good friends.

One day the door opened and in walked Jean, crying. Apparently three men attempted to rob her because they assumed she was carrying my drugs. We knew the identity of one of the men, and we were sure if we located him soon they would still be together. The three had a reputation of robbing other dealers, so it wasn't hard to locate them. Softy and I parked down the street from the hotel. Softy took the Louisville slugger from underneath the front seat, and we headed toward the entrance.

"Ain't going to be no mercy, Bro," Softy said walking ahead of me.

There was a large group of dangerous and sleazy characters loitering and hanging around the hotel. Inside the hotel was the usual crowd lingering in the lobby. When we reached the room, we could hear them talking through the wallpaper thin door. I took my 25 automatic from my pocket and injected a round into the chamber. Softy held the bat in both hands and kicked the door open making a loud bang, catching them completely off guard. Drug paraphernalia was on the dresser, and more than likely the drugs they had just used was taken in an earlier robbery.

All three stood there with their mouths open and eyes wide with fear; it was pay back.

"Softy, Iiii—" the oldest one tried to say.

His words were cut short. Softy swung the bat with both hands striking him on the arms as he tried to protect his head. The force dropped him to his knees and blood shot from his head like someone had suddenly turned on a faucet.

"Wee-Wee!" he yelled like a wounded animal.

I held the other two at bay with my 25, and Softy continued to swing the bat. Suddenly I recalled his words, "There ain't going to be no mercy." And he was true to his word. He then turned to the others screaming obscenities as the bat made contact with their flesh. When we left, blood covered the room.

We left the hotel at a fast pace, but no one said a word as we walked down the stairs and through the lobby. We got into the car and slowly drove away as if nothing had happened. It was just another day in the violent world in which we lived. We had gone over the edge, and we had lost control. Here, human life wasn't worth a nickel; it didn't mean any more than the time it took to produce it.

I continued to sell drugs trying to regain what I once had. Jean was pregnant again. My son kept growing. Softy was robbing major dealers for a living, and our time on the clock was running out fast.

On November 23, 1972, Thanksgiving Day, my daughter was born. She was the cutest baby girl I had ever seen. She had eyes and a mouth exactly like her mother, and she was my princess. Shortly thereafter my brother was in a shootout, and there was only a few minutes left on the clock before our time ran out.

One morning Jean and I came home about 5 a.m. The children were with her mother, and Jean was supposed to have been resting. She tried to convince me to get into a drug program, but I denied I needed help. Later as I lay in her arms, suddenly I had a premonition. I knew it would soon be over for me. I felt it; I saw it as plain as day. I knew I didn't have many more nights to hold her in my arms. I didn't know exactly how it would end, but I was sure it would end soon. The clock was still ticking, but there was absolutely nowhere else to go.

I opened my eyes one morning in 1973, and I saw only 3 seconds remaining on the clock. Then, it would all be over. But little did I know my troubles were just beginning.

Although it was always very brief, I saw Jean and the children almost daily. One evening when I went over, she was terrified. The police wanted to question me about a drug-related homicide in Maryland. They told her I was dangerous and I should turn myself in because they didn't want to shoot me on sight. One part of me said leave town, but the other part of me said I couldn't. If I could only see them for a moment each day, I had to take that risk.

One day I stood just inside a busy luncheonette on Fourteenth Street. Suddenly a deadly silence fell over the lunch room. A hand touched my left shoulder and when I turned, I saw the reason for the silence.

I faced two young black men in dirty blue jeans and cheap cotton shirts. Standing in the door was a third black man with a large afro and similar attire. But everyone knew they were not ordinary men. They were undercover police, and they were looking for a WANTED MAN!

"Cheese," the one with his hand on my shoulder said. It wasn't a question; it was a statement.

"Who? Cheese? I am sorry, but I've never heard of him," I said loud enough for everyone to hear.

"Then what's your name?"

"My name is John W. Pressley."

"Do you have any identification?"

"I certainly do." I reached inside my coat pocket and withdrew a long businessman's wallet. I produced the identification and gave it to him. For a moment he looked bewildered and confused. He took the wallet from my hand and examined it carefully. There was one piece of small paper with the name Cheese on it. When he saw it, his face lit up and he no longer looked puzzled.

"Get that poster from the car," he told his partner who was standing at the door.

He returned with a large wanted poster with my picture only a few months old. It said in large black print: WANTED, FIRST DEGREE MURDER, Prince George County, Cheese. They had their man. As they handcuffed my hands behind my back, I looked at the clock on the wall and the last second had expired; my time had finally run out.

I was interrogated by two detectives from Prince Georges County the following morning, and I went to court for arraignment on an old assault charge that I failed to appear in court on. A date was set for sentencing and I was transported back to the district jail.

When I arrived, it was as if time had stood still; nothing had really changed. I saw the same old faces, playing the same old games, and telling the same old stale lies. We thought we were ultra-slick and knew all the right moves, but we were still play acting, nothing more. We had taken a script that had been written, produced and designed precisely for us. All that was required for me to take a part was to be a good actor. You had to laugh when you wanted to cry. You had to be brave and demonstrate courage when you were literally frightened to death. When you were weak as creek-water, you had to practice deceit and mislead people into believing you as were strong as Samson and tough as nails. When you were beaten and tired and wanted to quit, you had to pretend you were as fresh as a daisy. And when you had lost and been defeated, you told yourself you were a winner and the victor.

Every now and then someone came along and told us to step out of the play. And when they did, we thought they were insane. Our parents told us not to play those parts because they were death scenes. Older brothers who had once walked that road advised us not to play those fatal parts. They told us they had played the same parts, but I know in playing them they were killed. Oh—they told us; we heard, but we didn't really understand. After all, we were the stars of the show and they were observers, watching from the audience.

Didn't they know we would give up anything rather than what we wanted to believe? Didn't they know they could tell us there was nothing to believe, prove it to us, but we would go right on believing? How could they tell us our whole world was a lie and our dream a fantasy?

Thirty days after I was in the jail, the detainer was lodged against me from Maryland. That same week I went to court to be sentenced for the assault charge. The judge recognized I was in deep trouble in Maryland and only sentenced me to nine months. I was shipped to Lorton awaiting the fight for my life in one of the most racist counties in the state.

Again, I recalled a passage from the book of Job. "Why died I not from the womb? Why did I not give up the ghost when I came out of the belly?" I had already died a thousand deaths, but I would have to die many more before I saw a ray of light.

11

954 Forrest Street

"The textbooks on criminology like to advance the idea that the prisoners are mentally defective. There is only the merest suggestion that the system itself is at fault ..."

George Jackson

IF YOU LOOK AT most prison populations, you'll see the vast majority of its inmates are black, and we will conclude from this observation that the majority of crimes are committed by blacks, and blacks commit far more crimes than whites.

If we reach this conclusion, and we often do, it is inaccurate. So again, equality under the law is still a myth.

It is impossible to enforce all laws against all lawbreakers. One survey by the president's crime commission reports that ninety-one percent of all Americans have violated the laws that could subject them to a term in prison. So what laws do you enforce and against which people? The question is simple. The laws are mostly enforced on the blacks, who also happen to be poor. Consequently, the poor are arrested more often, convicted more frequently, sentenced more harshly, and rehabilitated less successfully than the rest of society.

It took the Kerner Commission to tell the nation what we as black folks have known for centuries—America is indeed a racist country. Black prisoners in America are the victims of social injustice, and no other institution is free to practice racism and injustice more than the American legal system and its prisons. My ride from Prince Georges County to the Maryland Penitentiary was short. I sat with my face pressed to the small barred window looking out at the scenery as the van sped toward my final destination. I had no false illusions about my ride. Perhaps, it would be the last ride that I would ever take. As I viewed the scenery, I thought how strange everything and everyone seemed on the inside looking out.

I thought the penitentiary was located in Baltimore County, but it wasn't. To my surprise, it was situated in one of the inner city sections of Baltimore City. From a distance you could see the tall steeple ascending into the heaven like a picturesque post card. But once you reached the intersection of Forrest and Eager Streets, you saw a much different site. The picturesque post card became a nightmare; 954 Forrest Street was indeed a house of horror. It was built in the mid-1800s and is one of the oldest operating prisons in America.

When I exited the van and adjusted my eyes to the sunlight, the complete picture loomed into view. I'll be a monkey's uncle; they really chose a nice place for me to live, or perhaps die, I remember thinking. It was like I had gone on a journey back in time as I viewed the old dismal ancient structure. At any moment I expected a madman to charge out the door and down the steeps screaming, "Freddy is back!" Well, here I was; I had finally arrived home.

How many mothers and wives had lost their sons and husbands to these old walls? How many children had it made orphans? How many men had lost their minds here, and how many souls had been lost? These were the thoughts as I went behind the walls for the very first time. There was no band playing when I arrived; there was no welcome home sign hanging out front for me. No matter who you were on the outside, you were just another number, and the only time you mattered was during count time.

I had come to the end of the line, and it was the bottom of the barrel. Here were the most dangerous and worst convicted criminals in the state of Maryland; still, you were only a number. Here, men had controlled empires and allegedly sold millions of dollars worth of drugs a year, but that didn't count anymore. Here, men were convicted of crimes as heinous as decapitation and left enough dead bodies scattered over the state of Maryland to claim a private cemetery, but that no longer mattered either. In every sense of the word, prison life was hell! Here, only the strongest of the strong survived and the weak and feeble didn't stand a ghost of a chance. Here, you put your brains in a paper bag and checked it at the door. Your reputation, name, and criminal status was credited to yesterday's account, and your present status meant absolutely nothing. This was where you proved yourself each and every day; past deeds no longer counted.

The Maryland Penitentiary was constructed from the old Auburn prison system. Cell blocks were erected in tiers of cells placed back to back in tiers three feet, six inches wide. Under the Auburn system there was no communication allowed between inmates, and it was the administrator's philosophy that no change could take place until the prisoner's will was broken. Today, we are allowed communication, but it is still the philosophy of many that no improvement could begin until our wills were broken.

The prison system at its best has always been a failure. John Howard, perhaps the greatest of all penal reformers, was determined to learn first hand what prompted society to be so cruel to those who had erred against mankind. In his work State of Prisons published in 1777, he had a mental picture of a institution called a penitentiary, where real penitence could be encouraged among the inmates. It was Howard's theory that a program that consisted of work, education, and religion was the best design for reform and improvement.

Later, after the revolution, a group of men in Philadelphia organized a prison reform society to produce a decent system for reforming criminals. The Act of April 5, 1790 created the first modem penitentiary, changing the status of the Walnut Street Jail in Philadelphia. But their reform was short-lived. The increase in population and the general apathy made it difficult, if not possible, for this institution to maintain its reputation as a model. The good that men do is always offset by the evil of others.

Today, prison reformers are just about a thing of the past, but the same conditions that prevented those reformers from being successful are still prevalent to this day. By 1870 even the progressive prison administrators were convinced that no progress had been made. The penitentiary system as practiced then was admittedly a FAILURE, so it was in 1974, one hundred and four years later, that prisons were still a FAILURE.

My first stop inside the prison was the storeroom. It was located at the end of A Block next to the guard's desk. Enroute, I noticed convicts standing around on each tier landing and rushing up and down the long, busy tiers, and the noise was deafening. When I reached the storeroom, there were a dozen or so other convicts who had just arrived and were waiting to be processed. After we were processed, our next stop was the mess hall for dinner and then to the hospital. We had a brief examination, and we sat around for hours waiting for them to find room for us. In February 1974, the pen was so overcrowded that they didn't have room, and didn't know where to put us. After other inmates were shuffled around, the only available space was on segregation. But I was so tired it didn't matter if they had put me on the roof. All I wanted to see was a bunk.

The convicts were now called inmates, and the guards were called correctional officers. They no longer carried clubs; they had strict rules for discipline. Segregation was reserved for inmates serving time for violating institutional rules. Although we had violated no rule, this is where we were temporarily housed until space was available.

At this time segregation consisted entirely of the notorious Southwing. It was well after nine that night when we got there, and it was the ugliest sight I had ever seen inside a prison. It was filthy, foul, and stinking. The cell block was five tiers high with 26 cells to a tier. It had two sides, east and west. It was infested with rats, roaches, and pigeons. Trash and garbage were piled up on the first tier like a dump; it was terrible and looked worse than the city dump.

In 1974, overcrowding was becoming a major problem in the Maryland prison system. Younger black males were coming to prison with longer sentences and fewer were being released. The National Council on Crime and Delinquency (NCCD) released a report on our prison population: In 1850, we had an incarceration rate of only 29 inmates per 100,000 population. A short time later, the rate climbed to nearly 100 inmates per 100,000 population, and there it stayed—between 75 and 125 per 100,000—until about 1970. Since then it has doubled, and the trend shows no signs of abating.

To alleviate this growing problem, the state of Maryland began to construct more prisons. That was much easier than to address the cause of the problem; it was much easier to deal with the effects than to seek a solution to the cause. Remember, the system itself is seldom at fault.

Within a few days I got to know some of the inmates who were doing lock-up time. Most of them had been in the pen for many, long years. These men were considered by the prison officials to have serious disciplinary problems and some were considered mentally defective; and consequently, they did most of their time on segregation.

I became acquainted with two inmates in particular from Washington. They both had been incarcerated since the early '60s, and they were anxious to know all about the world that had passed them by. They wanted to know about the world that had come and gone while they spent a large portion of their lives, and all their youth, behind the walls in prison.

There was one inmate who came to his cell door early every morning and announced, "Roll Call." And he proceeded to call off a long list of names.

Then, there were some who came to their doors and entertained us each night with their comedy. This went on all night and it was almost impossible to sleep. If you didn11 sleep during the day, you didn't sleep at all. When the comedy was over, the singing began. Everyone wanted to be the Temptations.

"I got sunshine on a cloudy day."

"Doo-do-do-da-doo."

"You need more than sunshine," someone might yell, "You need to learn how to sing."

After two weeks, we moved from the Southwing to the Receiving Diagnostic Classification Center (RDCC). In those days, RDCC was still located in the pen. It consisted entirely of B block, and everyone who was sentenced in the State of Maryland had to come here to be classified. Once you were classified, they determined at which institution you served your sentence. Naturally with the length of my sentence, this was home. I was classified to A block and assigned to work in the kitchen. When I tried to protest, I was told I had two alternatives, the kitchen or segregation. Naturally I went to work in the kitchen.

When I went into population, it was still overcrowded, so I was temporarily housed on the death row tier with the inmates who had been sentenced to die. I only stayed there a short time and then I was moved to a regular tier. As I moved around in population, I discovered I was with friends from the training school, youth center, and Lorton. Their sentences ran from 50 years, to double life plus 50 years. And I thought I was the only one in trouble.

When the judge sentenced me to life, subconsciously I had given up, and it didn't take long for my action to reflect it. Soon I discovered I was only one out of the vast majority who felt the same way. OH—we would never tell you we had given up. You see, that wasn't cool; but our actions spoke it loud and clear. We drank homemade wine until we were no longer able to remember yesterday's deeds, or recall what day it was. We shot so much and so many different kinds of drugs we were virtually unconscious and sometimes foaming at the mouth. We sold death a mile long and gambled with our lives playing silly games, hoping someone would have the courage to put us out of our misery and end it all. But OH—we would never tell you we had given up!

Practically everything we did, our actions screamed kill me! Kill me because I don't want to witness another sunrise. It was as if an invisible dark cloud had settled over the pen and everything within its walls was dead or waiting to die. It was a graveyard if I had ever seen one. Our beds were our coffins; each of us had become a corpse, and all we needed was a single shovel of dirt to cover our graves. OH—but we would never tell you we had given up. We made our lips say we want out, but our actions betrayed us simply because there was no connection in our footprint and thinking. Somehow we always talked east but ended up going west.

Time passed rapidly. Years had come and gone (1974 through 1977) and all I did were the same things that had brought me to prison. I had allowed myself to become trapped into a prison way of existence, and all that interested me was a moment's worth of pleasure. I used drugs and alcohol to keep me from remembering, to ease my pains, and to help me forget about my yesterdays. I really thought my life was over and all that was left was the grave.

In 1977, the prison and administration gradually began to change, but we stayed behind because we liked the conditions as they were. We were caught up in our yesterdays, and we were much too wise to invest in tomorrow. How could we? With the lifestyles we lived, we realized that tomorrow for us might never come. And for many it didn't.

Mom came to visit me regularly with the kids. This was the part of prison life that I hated the most. Being separated from my family and children was hell. When I left for prison, my son was three and my little daughter was only six months. Now seeing them pained my heart, for I was not there with them to see them grow. They continued to grow bigger, yet I continued to see them as they were when I left.

The visiting room was extremely small. It was no larger than a match box, and on busy days you almost had to sit in another inmate's lap. Your visitors sat on one side of a divider, and the only time contact was permitted was upon arrival and departure. Once you took your seat, you were not allowed to make contact, not even for a second.

I had to emotionally prepare myself for each visitor from home. I would be so happy to see them but truly sad when they left. I sat and laughed with them for one hour but literally cried for days when they left. It is painful to see your children grow up at a distance. They grew inches with each visit and asked a thousand questions: Could they come downstairs and see where I lived? Was I getting enough to eat? When was I coming home? These questions kept coming, and I tried to answer them as honestly as I could. Every visit I told them how much I loved them, but I couldn't reach out and touch them, and I had to wonder if they truly understood.

Could they understand that as much as I loved them I couldn't be there with them to see them grow into adolescence and dry their eyes when they cried? Could they understand why they had to leave me behind after a visit; could they? Then why couldn't I return home with the family if my love was authentic and genuine? Each year they grew taller, older, and wiser, but I remained trapped in a world of yesterdays.

I hadn't seen Jean since I left Lorton in '73. I think she finally understood what I was trying to tell her when I last saw her; still, I couldn't stop thinking about her or get her completely out of my mind. At times I wondered who she could be with or what was she doing. On cold winter nights, thoughts of her warmed my soul and my cold lonely bed.

In 1977 I was charged with possession of five bags of drugs and received thirty days on segregation. Segregation was no longer in the Southwing; it had moved to C-Dormitory. But here the conditions were worse than the Southwing. It was murky and disgusting. Some cells had excrement smeared on the walls as well as on the bars. It was tarnished and musty, and many times we were lucky to get a shower once a week. One friend I knew would take a trash bag and put it in a large cardboard box and make a bathtub and take a bath. The food was served in foam cups ice cold, and you froze to death in the winter and roasted in the summer.

But the activities of the inmates hadn't changed one iota. They still slept all day and kept you up at night. And they still had the main characters to entertain everyone with their comedy and humor. We all had to find a way to laugh to keep from crying, and we laughed at each other. They talked about each other's family members, from their mothers, little sisters, and even grandparents. No subjects were barred when they came to their cell doors. When they got tired of playing the dozens, they told dirty jokes and sang till the sun came up.

Anything that was needed from another cell, or even another tier, was done by a process called fishing. You shredded a sheet and made a line, and you tied a weight or heavy object to the end. When you had to get something from another cell, you simply stuck your arm out the bars and tossed the line down the tier. Whomever it was to, they pulled it in and attached the object to the line and you pulled it back into your cell. All night you heard inmates hollering.

"Pull the line in."

"Where is it going?"

"Throw the line back down."

Mom and Daisy had joined the church, and mom continued to bring the children at every opportunity. I had other female friends to visit, but after all these years, my mind was still on Jean. I couldn't erase her from my mind no matter how hard I tried. When I went to sleep at night, she was with me. When I was intoxicated trying to forget, she was still with me. I just couldn't get her out of my mind.

James V. McConnell, a leading behavioral scientist, said, "We have but two means of educating people or rats or flatworms—we can either reward them or punish them…"

Make no mistake about it, the American prison system is not in the business of rehabilitation; it is in the business of punishing its victims and warehousing them. They hold them until they are made worst, then they return them to society where they have stored away the nightmares into corners of their minds, only to soon explode and do violence to themselves and others.

I began to see young kids come into prison sixteen and seventeen years old with long prison terms; they were disillusioned, hurting, and in pain. I saw guards who came to work with their only concern being to turn keys and pick up a paycheck every two weeks. They made a profit off our flesh, and every night they went home and thanked God for a system that rewarded their inefficiency. So we became empty shells, living but not being, looking but not really seeing, and hearing but not understanding.

Prison had conditioned us to be the best we could be in prison. We were conditioned to be the best dresser, be the best hustler, be the smoothest talker, and be the best actors. These were the status symbols in prison that verified we were the best in prison. We were conditioned to be a thousand things inside the walls of prison, but we gave no thought at all about anything on the other side. This was our home; the judges had made sure of that, so how could any of the things about the other side make sense to us? We were conditioned to believe that life meant never leaving here alive, and it was only a matter of time before death over took us all.

Two of my friends died from a drug O.D. (overdose) that summer. In order to survive, when we saw death snatch our friends, we had to harden our hearts and not give it too much thought if we wished to keep our own sanity. Luckily for us AIDS was unheard of in those days; if so, we all would have probably died from that terrible disease.

Every night when I lay down there was no guarantee I would see the morning sun, and when morning came I didn't know whether I would make it through that day. Soon those thoughts began to take its toll on me and all I thought about was death. I had been tried and convicted, so nothing or no one could help me now. I was afraid—afraid to live and afraid to DIE!

12

We Almost Made It

"No other experience, no other social phenomenon, can equal the traumatic effect of imprisonment, the total loss of all liberty."

George Jackson

"To put people behind walls and bars and do little or nothing to change them is to win a battle but lose a war. It is wrong. It is expensive. It is stupid. We can't just dump people in prison without trying to do something for them."

Chief Justice Warren Burger

EARLY ONE MORNING I stepped out of my cell, going to breakfast, into the middle of what I thought was a fistfight, but I should have known better. I must have been insane; no one had fistfights anymore.

Two inmates were swinging, poking, prodding, and jabbing repeatedly at one another. Both had long sharp prison made shanks. One was long and made in the fashion of an ice pick, and the other shank had a wide, flat edge made like a miniature sword. One inmate had a deep gash in his forehead and blood was pouring profusely down his face onto his shirt. Apparently the other inmate had been stabbed in the chest and abdomen because dark stains had turned his shirt blood red. Some inmates were trapped in the line of fire and were climbing the bars attempting to get out of danger. The inmate with the ice pick made a wild dash forward and I saw the point disappear deep into the other inmate's flesh.

"Ugh, You son…!" he said as he dropped to one knee on the tier.

The other inmate concealed the weapon under his shirt and rapidly moved to the end of the tier. He never looked back, but he should have. The inmate he had stabbed had many friends on the tier and was well-liked. Two of his friends had disappeared into a cell and now they had reappeared. They waited until their friend's attacker reached his cell, and they attacked him.

One of them raised an iron pipe in one hand and brought it down violently across the back of his head. Before he could respond, he struck again. Then, his partner pulled a small weapon from his pocket and began to puncture him with holes. When he realized they were trying to kill him, he began to scream for his life.

"Guard! G-U-A-R-D!"

A small guard ran on the tier with a walkie-talkie to his mouth repeating a code, "Ten-ten! Ten-ten!"

Soon the tier was swarming with guards. The injured men were rushed to the prison hospital on stretchers. I thought as I walked off the tier what a way to begin the day. Most normal people begin their day with a nice nutritional breakfast, a kiss from their spouse, and a hug from their offsprings. But not here in the pen. We weren't normal; were we? We began our day with hatred, rage, frustration, blood, and violence.

Prison in many ways punishes by creating an unpleasant and violent atmosphere, and such an atmosphere only causes more violence. Men are herded together like cattle, but in most instances cattle have more freedom than prisoners and sometimes they are treated more humanely; so this experience has a traumatic effect on our lives. We are afraid to strike out at those responsible for this condition, so we attack one another.

Sociologists and psychologists know that if you put a maximum amount of people into a minimum amount of space, you've created a hostile and unfriendly environment. We learned very early in our prison experience to mask our fears with aggressiveness. We masked our guilt by blaming others, and we turned off our true feelings and operated on the unnatural.

It was also here that I first heard the term zap-out. I had no idea the word referred to an individual who was mentally unstable. These were the real forgotten men in prison. They had spent so many years in prison that everyone had forgotten their names. They were very visible, anti-social, and had terrible hygiene.

Although these men were a small percentage of the population, they stood out like a sore thumb. Every morning when the inmates were busy going to their job assignments, it was common to see them picking up cigarette butts and rambling through trash cans searching for unwanted items and articles that were totally useless. There was one in particular whose name was Billy; some days he stood in the center of the baseball diamond gazing up at the sun until he literally passed out.

In addition to being visible, they were extremely anti-sociable. They had an imaginary line in their heads and under no circumstances would they cross it. No one wanted to have anything to do with them, including inmates and guards alike. It was a standard rule to be seated in the mess hall four at a table after you were served; however, this rule did not apply to them. It was not uncommon to see only one of them occupying an entire table alone. It was as though they had an unwritten code among themselves that made it unlawful for them to socialize.

But without a doubt it was their hygiene that made them untouchable. They never combed their hair, nor did they shave or shower. Many times inmates forced them to shower and clean their cells. On those rare occasions when they did shower, they put the same old dirty clothes back on, and the foul odor trailed them everywhere they went.

But who were we to look at them with scorn and contempt? In truth, we were no better than they were. None of us were considered normal. We were all forgotten men past the stage of rehabilitating. So we were just warehoused by society because no one knew exactly what to do with us. What do you do with men who society says can't be helped?

These were mental patients who were also trapped in a system that more or less disregarded them, simply because they didn't know exactly what to do with them either. Most of them were over-medicated with thorazine and left to wander around like zombies. Proper medical treatment was too costly and the time they needed to spend in the mental hospitals was too long, so they were shifted back and forth in the prison system like pawns on a chess board. It was pathetic; one look at them and you knew they didn't belong. They needed treatment, not prison. But on the other hand, it made perfectly good sense if you remembered that prisons don't restore, they damage. They don't mend, they break; and they don't build, they destroy.

One night I was finally able to fall asleep sometime around 2 a.m. Many nights I would fight sleep as long as I could because when I closed my eyes all I saw was death and the grave. I'd see myself lying in a coffin surrounded by my family and friends weeping for me. I would see my mother's face wrench in pain and her soul in anguish because a disorderly death had claimed her first born son. I would see my sister twisted in grief and pain, beating her bosom with her small fist trying to understand why all the men she loved so dearly slept in the bosom of the cold, ruthless earth.

I would see my son frantically crying as he tried to sit my lifeless body back up in the coffin.

"Get up daddy! You can do it. Don't let them take you so soon."

I'd see my daughter crying uncontrollably as she tried to understand life, mysteries, death, and the grave. I would see faces of friends as they looked with sympathy, saying goodbye. And finally I would break out in a cold sweat as I saw myself staring down at a face I no longer recognized.

"Help. H-E-L-P!"

I came awake and sat up in my bunk as if someone had poured a pail of ice cold water down on my face. What was that chilling sound? Suddenly I began to shiver because it was the call of death. But who was it calling?

"Help! Help!" The loud chilling voice came again. "Somebody call the guard."

I tried to convince myself it was a nightmare; it couldn't be real. But what was that smell! Was it smoke? I rolled out of my bunk and stood at my cell door and looked into the face of reality.

I began to shudder and my heartbeat increased and beat like a sledge hammer in my chest. Black clouds of smoke began to engulf cell block A, and I saw rainbow colored flames shooting out the bars like an incinerator. The cell block was now in an uproar, and everyone was yelling, crying and banging on the bars.

"H-E-L-P! H-E-L-P!" the shrieking voices continued.

I heard the sound of keys and walkie-talkies announcing the code ten-ten. Suddenly the screams were silent! We were rushed from our cells and the fire department was summoned. But for two inmates, it was much too late. We were told that when the firemen arrived they had to use shovels to scoop the remains of the men off the floor to put what was left in body bags.

An unknown enemy had sprayed their cell with a highly flammable liquid and ignited it. For them the fat lady had sung, and they died trapped in their cell without a fighting chance. The fire was so intense it bent the bars as if they were made of soft clay.

This was a tragedy, but who would really care? We're all inhuman anyway. Who would mourn their deaths, who would miss them, and who would shed a tear? We were all animals tossed away by society and written off as worthless losers and good-for-nothing lazy bone loafers. And any death, no matter how shocking, and how horrifying, or how hideous was more than we deserved or had a right to expect.

If you treat a human being like a dog or animal long enough, he will eventually behave like one. If you tell a child he is nothing long enough, he will accept it as truth, even if it is a lie.

In many instances prisoners are treated as being less than human; we are numbers not individuals. If guards used excessive force, society closed its ears to our cries, thus sanctioning brutality. We are forced to live in an environment where privacy is a dirty, four-letter word and eliminated in the name of security. If you use the toilet, your cell partner is forced to smell your stink. Even when you eat your meals, another inmate is sitting across from you, inches away staring down your throat. Inmates are forced to live closer in prison than a husband and wife living at home. The prison system demands us to live this close, yet we are not expected to exhibit any violent acts even when we don't have room to move or air to breathe.

There were a few prison officials who thought some of us could be helped, and they did what they could at times. But these officials were a vast minority, and their efforts went mostly unnoticed.

One day while working in the kitchen a female dietary officer made me aware of a small growth on my neck, and she advised me to see the doctor. But I had no intention of seeing a doctor, and every day I told her tomorrow—tomorrow. She was persistent until I finally saw a doctor. I was certain it was nothing. If anything it couldn't be more than a cyst.

When the doctor examined it, he wasn't sure what it was. Just to be on the safe side he scheduled me to see a specialist at University Hospital. I was very appreciative, but I was still certain it was nothing but a cyst.

Because of security reasons, they never give you a date for your appointment, so about thirty days later I was called back to the hospital. They were sending me to University to see the specialist. It was July 14, 1978, and this was my first trip beyond these walls since I arrived in February '74. I considered the ride a pleasure trip, and I sat back and enjoyed the scenery. I looked at all the pretty girls in short pants with desire in my heart and lust in my eyes. Behind the walls everything was dead, but on the other side, everything appeared different. The air was fresher and even the sun seemed to shine brighter.

The specialist wasn't sure what the growth was either, so he admitted me to the hospital for further tests. My mother came the following day and they explained to her my condition. They had to perform a minor operation to remove the growth. Although it was a minor operation, it was my first time being admitted to a hospital, and it would be my first time in an operating room.

I was put on the ninth floor in the security ward. The following day I remember mom walking me to the operating room, and when I woke up I was back in my room. I had a patch on my neck and it was slightly numb. I ate nice hot meals in bed, flirted with the attractive nurses, and watched color television. As soon as I thought everything was going well, things began to get serious.

The specialist sent the tissue to the pathologist and it was diagnosed as a CANCEROUS tumor. I had been able to handle anything in my life; come what may I could take it, but now I was afraid to death!

They had to perform an exploratory surgery to discover the location and cause of the cancer. I had a female doctor who was extremely kind, and the night before my surgery she made the unknown journey less difficult. She briefly explained all the details from A to Z.

Mom was there early that morning. I hadn't eaten any solid food for 24 hours and the nurse gave me a shot to relax me. I remember them taking me to surgery, and mom was there trying to keep me calm. Her motherly instinct told her I was frightened half to death, and she was right. She walked beside my bed as it was wheeled to the operating room and assured me it was going to be all right; it was August 8, 1978.

When I opened my eyes, I was in the recovery room. My stomach was on fire, and my mouth was extra dry. There was a wide patch covering my lower abdomen that extended to my upper chest, and every few minutes I complained that my stomach was burning.

Later they took me back to the security ward. Everywhere I went I was escorted by a guard. Shortly back in my room, mom was there. She sat for hours before she finally left, but I knew she would be back early the next day.

I thought the fight was over, but it had just begun. I was diagnosed as having cancer of the liver. My long period of drug abuse had destroyed my liver. I also found out later when they performed the exploratory that they removed my spleen. They referred me to the Baltimore Cancer Research Center (BCRC) for chemotherapy treatment twice a week.

Mom traveled back and forth from Washington every day. Nine days later something had gone wrong. They couldn't get a bowel sound, and if I didn't go back into surgery immediately I would die.

I could never had made it without my mother. Every day at noon I listened for the sound of her voice coming on the ward. She was at the hospital so much that many thought she was a hospital employee. I didn't think I was strong enough to go through another operation so soon, but I had no choice; it was do or die! She gave me the strength and courage I needed to face the darkness and uncertainty again. I was afraid, and the feeling I felt was total fear.

As I was being wheeled to the operating room by the attendants, mom was on one side and the guard was on the other. I kept repeating to myself, "I don't know about this one; I don't know about this one," and I really didn't. This time she didn't remain outside, she slipped into a hospital gown and came in with me. At that moment I realized I was in more trouble than they wanted me to know.

When they put me on the table, I looked at mom for what might have been the last time on earth, and I wanted to say so much to her.

"Mom," I wanted to say to her, "I've always loved you more above all others, and God could not have made a more perfect mom than you." Lying there I thought about all the love she gave us and the sacrifices she made. I remembered how she always put her children first, and herself last. I had an I. V. in my arm, and the anesthesiologist put something in the tube and told me to count to ten. I didn't make it; I was out.

When I opened my eyes in the recovery room, it was not like before. My stomach felt like a furnace. I tried to speak, but I had a tube in my mouth and couldn't produce a sound. I had tubes everywhere, and I was in severe pain. Because of the seriousness of my condition, I was placed in intensive care. The surgeon had to make an incision into the old surgical wound, and when I saw it for the first time, it was an ugly sight. The nurse had to change my bandage and dress my wound daily. When she removed the wide bandage, I had to quickly glance away. There were wire staples extending from my upper chest to my groin.

Back in the security ward my condition deteriorated, and I was placed on the critical list. Still, my condition got worse. I had complication after complication, and everything had gone wrong. I found out when it rained, it really did pour. After doing all they could medically, they had to tell mom there was nothing else they could do, and it was just a matter of time.

Death and I had a terrible fight. But this time I wasn't fighting for a title or championship. I was fighting for my life; winner take all. Mom was there approximately six or more hours each day. When everyone had given up, she held on to a faith that was unshakable. The best they could do was keep me full of drugs to ease my suffering and pain. I would doze off and wake to find her still at my bedside praying with a Bible in her lap. I would look at her and not understand why she hadn't given up on me long ago. I never caused her anything but grief and pain, but she never—never stopped loving me. I couldn't understand in spite of all I did why she always stood at my side.

On one hand, I was tired of fighting; I had no energy left. My temperature was so high they told her if it got any higher they would have to pack me in ice. I lay there in a cold sweat shivering uncontrollably. And she still held my hand and wiped my brow. Now I had to tell her goodbye, but how could I? How could I tell her I wasn't worth fighting for any longer when she had fought for me all her life?

"Ma, I am so tired," I whispered.

"I know you are; I know you are."

"I'm so tired I want to close my eyes and sleep forever."

"But you can't," she said. "Look how far we've come already."

I had a difficult time making her leave that night, and I understood why. Every night when she left she realized she might never see me alive again, and that was a heavy burden to bear.

One night I opened my eyes to find my room full of nurses shouting orders in a state of panic.

"Call his doctor; call his doctor!"

In my sleep I had been pulling the tubes from my nose and mouth, so they had to tie my hands to one side of the bed. I couldn't understand it. On one hand I wanted to end it, but on the other, when I thought it was all over I found strength from somewhere to fight back. I couldn't die a prisoner. I had to die a freeman; besides, there were too many things left for me to do.

One night when I woke up, the prison chaplain was standing over me giving me my last rites, but day by day I kept holding on. Each morning when my doctors made their rounds, it was a miracle I was still alive. Medically, I was supposed to have been dead, and they couldn't explain nor understand it. No one could understand except my mother.

After weeks of fighting, I woke up one morning to discover I felt one hundred percent better. When the doctors made their rounds now, they discovered my condition had greatly improved. They told mom that they didn't know what it was she was doing but to keep doing it. Each day I got stronger and stronger. One morning a young nurse came into my room to change my bedding and give me a shot. She was in her mid-twenties and had beautiful hair. She was very attractive and had a small waist and wide hips. Every curve she had was in the right place. Underneath her white pants uniform, I could see her pink underpants, and when she bent over my bed I got sexually excited. Without a doubt, I knew I had gotten better.

Almost every morning at five an equally attractive young girl would wake me to take blood. She was tall, slim, and had an ebony complexion. I recall one morning in particular shortly before I was discharged she woke me to take my blood. Normally the guard came in with her but he didn't this particular morning. She had on dark pants and a light blouse. Her blouse had a draw string at the neck with a large opening. She told me her name was Dianne, and she had a good sense of humor. When she bent over to take my arm, my eyes focused in the opening of her blouse. To my delight she was not wearing a bra, and I saw her small breast. I waited until she was leaving before I made a comment.

"Dianne, are you sure you don't take anything but blood?"

"What are you talking about?" she asked.

I knew she didn't understand, so I tried to give her a hint.

"Thanks for the view."

I guess she thought I was crazy because she still didn't understand what I was talking about, so I made it as plain as I could.

When she glanced down at her bosom, she finally understood. "Men! That's all you ever think about," she said as she walked out of the room.

I was discharged September 9, 1978. I had spent 57 days in the hospital and most of those days were spent on the critical list. When I got back, they kept me in the prison hospital for observation. Shortly thereafter, University sent me an eleven page bill for $20,051.93. I had good hospitalization; everything was paid by the state.

Twice a week I was taken to BCRC for chemotherapy treatment. They occupied the eleventh floor of University Hospital. Chemotherapy and radiation were the only forms of treatment for cancer patients that I had knowledge of at that time. I had always associated cancer with old age, but all I saw coming for treatment were middle-age patients, young patients, and even children. Perhaps this disease had claimed the elderly population. Whatever the reason, I didn't have to be a detective to discover the statistic rate of cancer victims was extremely high. As a matter of fact, it was almost certain death.

To my surprise, the staff and patients were polite, friendly, sympathetic, and treated me kindly even though I was always chained and shackled.

"Must you keep him in that condition?" they asked.

"It is prison policy," the guards replied.

"But it is two of you, and you both have guns. Besides where can he go?"

Still they replied, "It is prison policy."

But while I was being treated, they demanded the cuffs be removed, and they removed them, however, they let it be known that the security of a prisoner superseded any medical attention they needed, even if it meant a prisoner's life.

The treatment left me nauseated, faint, and vomiting. And every time I combed my hair large patches came out in the comb. In a matter of days, I was almost completely bald.

Less than one year after treatment a miracle happened that I couldn't understand. The doctors couldn't find any trace of the cancer; they were amazed. They checked and double-checked, and still they could find no trace of any cancer. After they were absolutely certain, they discontinued my treatment; it was no longer necessary.

I was discharged back into the prison population. In a matter of days I was running again. It was 1980 and I was still playing a fool's game looking back at yesterday. The same advice I had once given Softy I found myself completely ignoring. It is no wonder he never listened; I never took my own advice.

About four o'clock one morning, pain in my lower abdomen woke me from my sleep. It was a burning pain so excruciating I could hardly move. Death was attacking me without a warning! I tried to get out of bed, but I couldn't stand up. I tried to yell, but my voice rose no more than a whisper.

Luckily for me a guard was making his rounds. He saw that I was ill, and I was taken to the hospital on a stretcher. The only medical personnel on duty was a nurse, and she didn't know what to do. She thought it was a virus, but I was sure she was wrong. She admitted me to the prison hospital to see the doctor when he arrived that morning.

All I could do was lie in a fetal position across the bed. I tried several times to drink water, but each time I would vomit. They could not give me anything for pain because they didn't know what the problem was. When the doctor arrived and examined me, I was rushed to University.

I was in so much pain that I thought I would pass out at any moment. When the doctors examined me and took X-rays, they told me I needed surgery immediately or I would die. Every time I was in trouble or pain the first word from my lips was MOTHER! I instructed them to call her and she was on the way.

Again, she went with me to the operating room. This would be the third time they had to make an incision in my abdomen and I was doubtful whether I would survive this one. My operation lasted almost eight hours. I had a lower bowel obstruction, and they also had to remove six feet of my intestines. The doctor said it was the worst case he had ever seen. It looked like someone had cut me open and packed my stomach with cement. Three days and nights I stayed in intensive care, and half the time I was unconscious. For three days and nights mom sat there with me fighting once again. The doctors tried to convince her to go home and get some rest, but she wouldn't leave me. As patients were dying in the night, mom would pull the curtain around my bed as if trying to keep death away from me.

After three days I was moved to the security ward. The staff of nurses was almost the same, and they were surprised to see me back. Four to five days later I was discharged back to the pen.

Man is born but one way, but there are thousands of ways in which he can die. From the moment I opened my eyes in the morning until I closed them at night, I continued to play Russian roulette with my life. It didn't make sense. One minute I welcomed death, yet the next minute I wanted to live. I was never satisfied with anything, including myself. I was dissatisfied and never content. No matter how good I was, to myself, I was never good enough. What would it take for me to understand that the grass is not always greener on the other side, and just because an apple was red, that didn't necessarily mean it was sweet? What would it take for me and so many others to say that enough was enough. Were we really inhuman like society said? Had prison turned us into animals and made us live like beasts?

One morning shortly after eight I was leaving the kitchen. As I approached the fence separating yards one and two, I noticed a group of inmates slowly running from A Block; there were five men carrying a green bench. On the bench was an inmate sitting up holding the back with both hands. He had his back to me so I couldn't see his face. My first thought was that he was having an epileptic attack. A guard stood outside the shack and said into his walkie-talkie, "…One yard to the hospital, one yard to the hospital, you have an emergency on the way, emergency on the way!"

When they reached me, they set the bench down for a second to get their breath. For the first time I saw who it was. It was an inmate who had grown up in prison. At one time he was the youngest inmate in the system. He had been sentenced to life as a teenager (thirteen) for the robbing and killing of a bus driver. He was a violent inmate who thought he knew all the answers. He was also given an additional 33 years for killing another inmate in 1976. Now, here he sat holding onto the back of a bench with his prison shirt soaked in dark, thick blood.

I looked into his eyes and there was nothing bad nor tough about him now. All I saw was fear and death. He was shaking, trembling, and afraid. At short intervals he gagged and vomited thick, black blood. He had been stabbed with a sharpened screwdriver.

"Aha-a-!" He opened his mouth wide and gagged and vomited again, then said, "Don't let me die—don't let me die!"

I picked up one end of the bench and we rushed him to the hospital as fast as we could run. The nurses and doctors were waiting in the dispensary. We set the bench down and then they ushered us from the room.

"Don't let me die; don't let me die!" These were the last words I heard him say. On the way out, higher prison officials were rushing in. But it was too late. Too late for them and much too late for him. He died one hour later, and there was no one to cry for him. To many people, his death was good news. They said he got what he deserved, but if that was truth, we all would have been dead long ago.

Mom continued to bring the kids, and they continued to grow before my eyes. In my mind they had stopped growing when I came to prison, and it was hard for me to see them any other way, except as still babies. We never discussed Jean too much. She was that part of me that I kept locked away in the secret chambers of my heart and soul.

The greatest war that has ever been fought is not on the battlefield, but in the heart and soul of man, good versus evil and right versus wrong. At times I got tired of playing foolish games, and I began to think more about my children. If someone asked them what had their father done, what could they tell them? What had I achieved, or who had I really helped in life? What could they tell them about their father that would make them beam with pride? I stood in the middle of the battlefield being pulled by two opposing forces, but the evil forces were winning the war as they always had.

One day I looked back and couldn't believe how many years I had spent in prison. The years passed so swiftly and many events had taken place behind these walls.

On September 17, 1982, a 21-year-old inmate was found hanging from the iron bars with a bed sheet knotted around his neck. Apparently he had given up. One day in prison life is too much for some to bear, so he sought eternal rest from this hell by ending it all with his own hands.

In 1983, three inmates escaped by overpowering two guards, took a captain hostage, threatened to kill him and another guard, fired gunshots inside and outside the prison, and escaped carrying three shotguns, two pistols and a walkie-talkie. Later one was killed in a hold-up attempt, and the other two were recaptured. However, one was transported to New York and later killed in another daring escape attempt. On October 6, 1984, a prison guard was fatally stabbed by an inmate on segregation.

Some nights when I went to sleep I still had dreams of Jean. The dreams of her never lasted more than a few minutes and she was gone; she seemed to disappear back into the darkness like a shadow. Why did she come and go so suddenly? Was it because I was lonely and needed so desperately to see that special smile, that special touch, or to hear that special voice that could still tie knots in my stomach after all these years? Out of my loneliness she crept into my cell and let me taste the sweetness of her lips, and when she left, the scent of her perfume engulfed my cell filling my nostrils. Was this her way of letting me know we were still together by an unbroken common bond? How could my soul find peace and tranquility in dreams of her; dreams that last for only a moment?

Our women are on our minds a great deal of the time. We daydream and fantasize about our first and last embrace. It is something about the opposite sex that makes a man feel whole and complete and more human. This trait is absent from our presence in prison, so we play games with our minds and fantasize and close our eyes at night and make love to our women long distance.

The clock of life is wound but once, and no one has the power to tell just where the hand will stop. So don't waste this precious time, and let us place no faith in tomorrow, for the clock may then be still. For so many of my friends the clock had stopped ticking and become still. So many have died from violence, disease, and drugs. When they died, who do you think mourned for them? And how many do you think had to be placed in a pauper's grave? Now as I glance back, I realize what a waste their deaths were; what a waste of human potentials.

My friends died of an illness not entirely their own, but an illness that was deeply ingrained in our American society. Beyond these walls it was said that Avis "tries harder," Maxwell House was "good to the last drop," and Ivory soap was "99 and 44/100% pure." Many companies and individuals became wealthy because the public believed these slogans; people were affected by what they heard.

In prison, we are told we are nothing and will never amount to anything. We were losers, rejects, and castaways, and we were locked out and away from society. The only time we made the news was when we killed guards or one another or attempted to escape over the wall. So we too were affected by what we heard.

We were told that to mourn was to be blessed, but did that mean out of darkness could come the dawn, that out of grief came joy, and that out of rain came a rainbow? Drugs had become a way of life for America, just like apple pie and baseball.

As I thought about my life and the lives of so many other prisoners, one theme kept reoccurring over and over in my mind: *We Almost Made It*. This theme exposed our lives before the world to what we had become.

"WE ALMOST MADE IT"

This is the story of our lives; isn't it? We almost made it. But if we miss by an inch, we miss by a mile. This is the story of our lives.

If we have four dollars in our pocket and the price is $4.01, then four dollars just won't do. This is the story of our lives.

We always seem to be one day late and five cents short, just to say, we almost made it! But almost never was nor is, good enough. We've lived all our lives coming within inches of our very best dreams, but they were plastic and artificial dreams locked inside our heads and hearts, but in reality they could never be real. But, we almost made it. Didn't we? Didn't we almost make it, man? This is the story of our lives.

Hey I Check me out. This is my story, and 1 am for R-E-A-L! 1 was one of the biggest dealers in the city; they called me mister, and I was the man. I had a Benz since I was fifteen, and I had gold ropes and diamond rings and the best of everything. I had an organization and we did business like IBM.

But if I could have only lasted six more months, I would have been untouchable, and I would have made it. But the feds had me under investigation. They gave me 20 years and a $50,000 fine. But if I could have only survived six more months, six months! Well, I almost made it. This is the story of our lives. We almost made it; didn't we?

Well! This is my story. I was a ^tick-up man, and I made my living with a 357, and it too was for real. I took $250,000 from the National Bank, but I was later betrayed by my best friend and rap-partner. So I made a deal and gave the money back, and *they only gave me a dime and let me do it with the state. For twenty-four hours, I had it all. Two-hundred and fifty grand! I had the whole world in my hands. But now 1 sit behind bars that are surrounded by walls, just to say, I almost made it. Well I did; didn't I?*

I was a confidence-man, I was a burglar, I was a thief. It doesn't matter what we were; our stories were the same. We almost made it; didn't we? Didn't we all? This is the story of our lives. We almost made it.

If he hadn't snitched, if 1 had gone left instead of right, if I had one more day, if darkness hadn't fallen so soon. But if—if—if... "if" is a word of fifty million and "if" is never good enough.

We came so close—so close. We live our lives to say in the end, "We almost made it." We spend our entire lives trying to play the game called catchup. And when we do, it is time for them to take us to the cemetery.

There, the grass will probably be green. The day warm and the sun bright. And there we '11 be... We almost made it.

Perhaps when they lower our lifeless bodies into the bosom of the cold earth, maybe someone will be there to shed a tear for us. Or perhaps on that day, they will sit in a bar drinking double after double trying to forget the pain and anguish we've caused them in life. And tomorrow, they will have forgotten that we ever existed.

And this is the story of our lives. We almost made it. Didn't we? Didn't we almost make it, MAN?

Cheese

13

The Resurrection

"For great is the mercy toward me; and Thou has delivered my soul from the lowest hell."

Psalm 86:13

THE SYSTEM HAS ADOPTED the theory that says, in effect, if you can't change prisoners for the better, we will sentence them to longer sentences and will hold them much longer. As a result of this theory, conditions of overcrowding are so severe that they have literally run out of space.

According to the Bureau of Justice Statistics, Maryland was one of the 11 states where the prison population increased by 20 percent or more and this figure was cited ten years ago. In 1973, the prison population in Maryland was 5,799. Years later in 1980, that figure went to 7,731 and in 1981 it climbed to 9,335. That meant from the year of 1980 to 1981 there was a 20.7 percent increase in the Maryland prison population. (A number of inmates sentenced to state facilities were held in county jails because of overcrowding.)

The tougher policies and stiffer sentences by the system and society help to explain why prisons have run out of room for prisoners. The system was sure that if the prison population increased the crime rate would decrease and society would become much safer. But in 1980, according to nationwide correction's department statistics, the crime rate increased by only 7.3% nationwide, but the total number of people incarcerated increased by 100% because of mandatory and longer sentences.

Another reason for the increase in prison population was due to more strict parole guidelines. Between 1977 and 1988, the percentage of inmates who left prison on parole fell from almost 72 % to only 43%. In many cases when these inmates were granted parole, they had served almost the entire length of their sentences, so the parole board would now give the parole to make it look good for statistics.

The taxpayers are somewhat confused as to what they want. The get-tough policy has proven to be extremely costly. Currently, 13 billion dollars per year is spent on U.S. prisons. If this increase continues, and I believe it will get worse before it gets better, the cost will be an additional 35 billion dollars over the next five years to build and operate more prisons. Today, prisons are becoming the fastest growing industry in America.

But this no nonsense and hard-nosed conservative approach to crime is not the solution to the crime problem; it never was. The authorities point out that this approach only causes a "sticking effect" where the prisons become more crowded even if the number of admissions doesn't change. If we cannot cure the AIDS problem by building more hospitals, why do we think we can solve the crime problem by building more prisons?

If society and the system seriously wanted to do something about the crime problem, they could. If they took a massive effort to turn prisons into rehabilitative correction centers, the crime rate would drastically decrease overnight. But it is sad to say they are not interested in rehabilitation, they simply want punishment no matter what the expense!

Close your eyes and die. Give it up; it is all over. There is no finish line; there is no Promised Land. The dream you have been living was an illusion, and it existed nowhere but in your distraught and confused head.

It was late in 1984, and I was still playing games and wearing a mask. Every morning as soon as my feet were on the floor, I would put on my mask and decide what game I was going to play for the day. I had a mask and game for each occasion. There were so many masks and games I often got lost and forgot who I really was. I could play games so well I could forget I was in prison, but I couldn't play so well that I could forget about yesterday.

I couldn't believe how big my son had gotten. Although he was now 15, he was over six feet tall and weighed over 200 pounds. Every time I saw my children it made me realize how much I really loved them and how much time I spent away from them. Jean had been shot in the neck. Annette had died of cancer, but the most tragic news of all, my son was beginning to live the lifestyle that I had lived and brought me to prison. He was becoming more like me, and I had promised he never would.

My first parole hearing was less than two years away, but I didn't give it a second thought. I was successful in deceiving my mother; she really thought I had gotten myself and life together. More than anything else in the world she wanted to believe that. She was certain after those bouts with death in University Hospital, even I wasn't foolish enough to resume my former lifestyle, but she was wrong. All her life she had only seen the good in me. She had come from that rare breed of parents that truly believed their children could do no wrong. If they did, they were justified and should have not been provoked.

Lying to mom was beginning to disturb my conscience, and I began to feel guilty, and it was getting harder and harder to lie to her. There was a war being fought on the battlefield of my soul, and sometimes I really felt as though I had had enough, but other times I felt as though I needed a little bit more.

Every morning the curtains would slowly rise on the stage of our lives. We would rise from our beds, shine our shoes and crease our britches, and move toward center stage. What mask shall we wear today, what game shall we play? How many lies will we have to tell today to protect our true identity? None of us were able to stop long enough to see what was really real. If we did, we would have seen that life was real, suffering and pain were real, and games were only an illusion. Prison cells were the results of the games we played; misery and death were the fruits of our labor. This was a fact, and this was real!

I had been in prison a long time now and this is what I have seen. I have seen men come into prison with a sound mind, but suddenly go out to lunch (become mentally ill and unstable) and never come back again. I have literally seen babies, 16 and 17, come into prison and get caught up in prison vices and lose their lives and go out the back door in a black body bag. I have seen young men come to prison with 20/20 vision and in perfect health. But over the years they need glasses to see, their teeth fall out, and their hair turns gray before your very eyes. These were facts; these were truths, and this was REAL.

Jackie and Hardy were two of my friends who started attending church. They went to Bible study, Chuck Colson seminars, and all other religious activities. As a result, I began to see a gradual change in their lives. They were far from being saints, but I could definitely see a change in these men's lives. Occasionally they invited me to attend church with them, but I would give them some flimsy excuse and look at them as if they were crazy. CHURCH! Me! I despised Christians. The greatest evils in the world had always been committed in the name of God and love, so I wanted nothing to do with their religion.

Christianity is not appealing to black men, especially black men in prison. First, we see a portrait of a man with blond hair, blue eyes, and pale skin, and we associate this figure with the same man who oppresses black folks, discriminates against black folks, and murders black folks without a just cause. This figure becomes an object of our hatred and we want nothing to do with this God.

We see this image hanging on a cross after being betrayed by the very ones He came to save, and we can't help but to cry out with the scribes and elders, "He saved others; Himself He can't save..." So this event that is unmatched by any event in recorded history becomes a symbol of defeat, not victory. Now when we see this cross, we flee in fear because it symbolizes defeat, suffering, slavery, and death.

If that was not enough, Jesus is too often portrayed in a feminine manner. Although the robes that He is dressed in are in accord with His time and customs, the colors are primarily reserved for females; men don't wear those colors. If this was designed, it worked successfully, because black men ran from Christianity as if it was bad news. Also, the churches had a membership where the females were a majority and the men were a minority, so this was another reason for men to stay away. Our egos and masculinity were involved, and we couldn't dare have them questioned or misunderstood.

But the longer I saw these men stand, the more I admired them. I saw something in them that I really wanted, but I was still too weak and made excuses. I had misjudged them. I thought they were weak, but they were really strong. You had to be strong to be a Christian in prison. You had to be strong not to wear a mask, and you had to be even stronger to step out of the great play. Perfection was not a characteristic of human nature. No, these men were not perfect; they were just a group of men who had grown tired of the old nothing way of life and were desperately trying to get their lives in order, and it was working.

I had heard you can lead a horse to the well, but you can't make him drink. As humorous as it sounded, there is a great deal of truth in that humor. Prison can offer an inmate the incentive to change; prison can provide the opportunity for a quality education, and make it mandatory for them to attend school if they don't have an eighth grade education. Prisons can mandate self-help organizations with outside sponsors and volunteers. But until an inmate makes up his own mind that he wants a change or a better life, that change can never be made; and no progress is possible. It is often when he hits the bottom that he will begin to look up. For me, I had hit the bottom; it just took me a long time to realize it.

At times I called my children on the phone, and occasionally I would talk to Jean. Their voices would ease my pain and their laughter soothe my sorrows. The first time I heard Jean's voice, I didn't even recognize her.

"Jean, is that really you?" Just at the sound of her voice thousands of emotions began to surface. I tried to recall how many years it had been, but it seemed like a lifetime ago. It had been so long, but her voice was still like a sweet symphony in my ear. I talked with her for a long time and then I heard her say.

"Cheese, why is it every time that I talk to you, you make me believe everything is going to be all right?"

"Because it took me a long time, Jean, to learn we have to have hope. We must have hope that tomorrow will be better than today. We have to have hope because without it, we die."

I told them all how much I loved them, and then I said goodbye. That night I closed my eyes and relived every moment I had spent with them, and I thought about freedom.

I thought about large spacious rooms without doors and windows that never closed. I thought about children doing their latest dances full of energy and laughter. I thought about the smell of a summer scent when the flowers were in bloom. I thought about FREEDOM, and suddenly my yesterdays were so very far away.

Somewhere something had gone wrong with us. We were all in trouble and needed help, and we didn't need it tomorrow, we needed it now and in a hurry. If we continued to play foolish games, the handwriting was printed on the wall in boldface letters, death. It seemed that life should have taught us that yesterday and tomorrow don't count; all that was important was the here and now. It didn't matter how you began the race, but it did matter how you finished.

It was 1985, my forty-first birthday was fast approaching and I felt just like Mathusala. It was said he lived on earth over 900 years, but there is nowhere in recorded history where he ever did anything. Until this point I had lived 40 years in vain, 40 years of an empty, hollow and fruitless life. For some reason I began to give serious thoughts concerning these matters. They nagged at my conscience with a steady and forceful frequency.

After celebrating my birthday with booze and drugs around the clock, I sat on my bunk, dreary and tired. I was tired of living, tired of dying, tired of life, tired of prisons, tired of booze and drugs, and tired of a nothing way of life, a life I could no longer live. I got on my knees and just above a whisper I said, "Lord, I am so tired, and I can't live this life any longer; enough is enough." I had no idea how long it would last, but I asked God to help me. I knew I didn't deserve to live, but still I asked Him to help me, and I waited to see the results.

Sunday came and passed and I didn't use anything. When night fell, I still was clean. There was a power in me that I never felt before, and for the first time in my life, I didn't have the desire to drink or use drugs. I told my friends I was turning over a new leaf, but they only laughed like I was crazy. They might have believed anyone else in the prison but me. They said nothing could help me, not even God.

Some friends are like crabs in a basket. When they see you trying to get out, they will pull you back down. As long as you remain content to wallow in the filth, you are admired by your peers. But once you attempt to better your miserable condition you are no longer loved, but despised. If these were really friends, I was better off without them.

Monday morning came and I was still clean. Every morning I listened to my favorite radio program from 6 to 10; it was WBGR, 860 AM, and its hostess was Pastor Naomi Durant. I had been listening to her program for years. No matter what condition I was in, her program never failed to bring me peace.

It was October 1985, one week after my birthday, and it would prove to be a day that I will never forget as long as I live. I was busy preparing lunch and I was in the room alone. It was 9:45 a.m., and the pastor had announced the altar call. Listeners were calling in having their names and the names of loved ones placed on the altar. Suddenly I heard voices begin to sing.

"C-O-M-E, un-to Jesus."

For some strange reason this song and lyrics caught my full attention. It was the Rev. Charles Nick, Jr., and the title of the song was "Come To Jesus."

As the song continued to play, I turned up the volume with my ears to the speaker. Something was taking place that I didn't understand. All of my life I had heard other people talk about it, but I never—never believed it was true. It was their imagination or lies. It was a mental image created by the mind and couldn't exist outside itself. They were outright lies told by superstitious people and were handed down, generation after generation to keep people looking for their pie in the sky. It had to be; there was no other explanation. There was no existing power or force in the universe that was able to do the things described. But my ears were glued to the radio, and I was in a trance and couldn't move.

> *"Come, un-to Jesus, while you still have time.*
> *Come, un-to Jesus, make up your mind.*
> *He will make your life brand new*
> *He will take care of you.*
> *Come, un-to Jesus, while you still have time."*

Without a warning I felt a sensation and warm feeling at the crown of my head. Slowly, very slowly it began to move down my body. As it moved, I felt a tremendous weight being lifted from me.

"Come, un-to Jesus, while you still have time."

All I could do was sit there and tears fell from my eyes like a flood, tears of joy and tears of relief. I knew what it was. It was not my imagination. It had not been a lie. It was the unseen hand of Almighty God saving the world's biggest sinner from torment, misery, and hell. I had been wrong; He was not dead nor was He a figment of the imagination. He was alive, and His spirit was entering into my heart. It was that very moment that I knew everything was going to be all right. I knew there would be no more dying for me. There would be no more booze, drugs, and living a lie. There would be no more masks to wear and games to play. For the first time in years I could be for real with others and myself. Tears—tears wouldn't stop flowing because I was sure I had died for the last time.

When the song ended, I ran to the phone and called my sister and all I was able to say was, "Sis, you don't have to worry about me anymore." I couldn't explain or put into words my experience. I kept repeating, "You don't have to worry anymore." Then I called my mother and repeated the same words, "You don't have to worry anymore."

What makes an inmate want to change? What makes him want to do right? Most of his life he has developed a pattern that deviated from the accepted norms of society. Many inmates will tell you that their actions were right, and it was society that was wrong; so why should they want to change now?

What can make an inmate change his present thoughts and behaviors? What can make an inmate think differently about life? In an article by D. K. Pace, President of Christian Jail Ministry, he lists some motivating factors.

One of the most important factors that motivates inmates is maturity. Studies show there is a correlation between higher age groups and a reduction in the number of repeat offenders. In other words, as people mature they commit fewer crimes. Today, crimes seem to be a young man's game. The older inmates now in prison are not new arrivals but most have already been there for many years.

Another strong motivator is fear. Every prisoner is afraid of dying in prison. You don't have to have a life term to die in prison. You can have six months or six days and die in prison by an act of violence or a natural cause. But fear is the same for all criminals according to Mr. Pace. Certain criminals react or respond differently to fear, and it seems to be a more powerful motivator among "white collar" criminals. They fear losing the respect and esteem of their families and friends, but "fear of punishment has a limited deterrence among drug-related and violent crimes."

Another powerful motivator that exists but goes mostly unnoticed or ignored is spiritual conversion. Granted, a lot of religion in prison is no more than what is known as crisis intervention. This is where we seek God only when there is a crisis in our lives, but once the crisis is over, so is our religion. We can develop a crisis-to-crisis spirituality where we can cry out, "Hey God, remember me? You got me out of a tight spot last year, but now I think I need You again."

But there are real genuine conversions that take place, even behind the walls in prisons. These sincere converts do not need a crisis to pray; they pray because they really love God. When a person is actively involved in church, fewer crimes are committed.

Religion can have a two-fold effect on the prison population. Emphasis on religious programs in prison can help turn some inmates from future crimes, and they can return to the communities from which they came and be a prime source to the inner-city youths and reduce the future inmate population.

It is sad to say that very little funding is spent on religious programs in prison. The system will spend $20,000 a year to keep an inmate in prison, but they will not spend $10,000 to help keep him out and make society a safer place to live. But remember, prisons gave up on rehabilitation programs long ago. Today, they are used as a source of punishment and warehousing.

It was October 7, 1985, when God saved me, and all my doubts and fears left. No matter what was to come into my life, come what may, I was certain everything was going to be all right. I didn't realize it then but all eyes were on me. I had to be playing a game. I had to have an angle. I had to have a secret and selfish motive; I couldn't be sincere. It just wasn't possible; there was no such thing as miracles.

I took out my Bible and began to read," …out of the belly of hell cried I, and Thou heardest my voice." I listened to the gospel tapes and recordings mom had sent. The desire for drugs and booze completely left me and I stopped using profane language, but I had more areas in my life to still work on. I couldn't wait for Sundays to attend church. Every day I spent hours on the phone with my sister talking about things I read in the scriptures. In a few months her bill was over $1,600, but she insisted I continue to call. She didn't even intend for me to know about the bill.

Thanksgiving, Christmas and New Years passed, and I was still holding on, and I was getting stronger spiritually each day. On February 2, 1986, I had my first parole hearing. Parole for a lifer in the state of Maryland is a difficult task, to say the least.

Based on information obtained by the families of Prison Coalition from the Department of Public Safety and Correctional Service, as of April 1, 1990 there were 1,135 inmates serving life sentences. During the past decade, 65 lifers have been granted parole. Fifty lifers have died while in custody, during the same period. Sixty-three of the paroled lifers were released by former Governor Hughes. Governor William D. Schaefer has only paroled two. Those lifers had served an average of 19.7 years. The average age of lifers, at the time of release was 45.6 years.

Traditionally, the parole commission has required lifers (once they have achieved statutory parole eligibility) to progress to lesser security for testing in minimum and prerelease programs. Often the parole board will give a series of short set-offs (one or two years) to keep inmates eligible for these programs.

Once the Parole Commission is satisfied that the inmates have been sufficiently "tested," they will order a post-sentence (really a pre-parole) investigation and psychological evaluation. The case is then reviewed by the whole commission to determine if referral to the Governor is justified. As stated previously, only TWO have been granted parole.

Three weeks later I received my decision." ...the panel felt that Mr. Cheese needs to spend more time in maximizing his educational background. He presently has a 10th grade education and we urge him to at least get his GED certificate. His skills in the field of modified diet, along with a GED, will make him marketable upon release to the community."

"OPINION: We feel that parole is premature at this point and that Mr. Cheese should be reheard in 8/89. This will allow him ample time to continue to make the necessary progress that is needed before he is given consideration for parole."

All the time I had spent behind these walls, I had not once given serious thought about going to school and getting an education. It was ironic that our ancestors and forefathers sacrificed all they had so that one day we would be afforded an opportunity to receive an education. In the dark day of chattel slavery it was against the law for a black to be caught with a book. They had to often steal away in the darkest of night to read the worn and frayed pages of a handbook by the light of the stars and moon, because they had a thirst for education. Today, their dreams had come true, and we were provided that opportunity even in prison, but we made a million ignorant and foolish excuses why we didn't need it. To us their dream was nonsense, and their proud, rich blood soaked the soil of the Mississippi mud in vain.

Later I went before the institutional board to review my status, and the board recommended transfer to the Maryland House of Correction (MHC). I noticed most of my friends still playing games. They had developed a philosophy of just wanting to get by. They had no priorities or directions in life, and they had stopped dreaming long ago. They had no hope, so they continued to die each night. Prison was getting worse, not better.

On March 10, two inmates were found hanged in their cells. One was Thomas Mann, serving three life sentences plus 1,080 years, who was found in cell block A. The other was Joseph Roberts, who was found hanging by a bed sheet from a light fixture in his cell on segregation.

In prison the innocent suffers with the guilty. But everyone in prison is not guilty, and everyone in society is not free. There are millions of people who carry their prison around behind their ears, and it is called the mind. They have a multitude of habits that would not allow them to be truly free. Solomon summed it up centuries ago when he said it was all "vanity." The things we lie for, cheat for, steal for, and even kill for, aren't they all vanity?

I had to spend a lifetime living a life of whys and regrets. But now I was able to stand in the midst of confusion and have peace. That emptiness was gone and in its place was a fullness that kept me overflowing with unspeakable joy. When mom asked me how I was doing, I could look her in the eyes and not have to lie. It was as if I was looking out at the world for the first time, and everything was crystal clear.

On June 6, they told me to bring my property to the storeroom; I was being transferred to the MHC. I said goodbye to my friends. Many I realized I would never see again in life. The vast majority would continue to play games with their lives until death struck its final blow, sending them home to a resting place in the earth. No one would ever know they existed, and fewer would remember their names. But it didn't have to be this way. Help was here, and all you had to do was ask God; He could give us a satisfaction and contentment that no money, drugs or fame could buy.

Two other inmates boarded the van with me for the MHC. I had spent twelve years behind these walls, and it was a miracle I was leaving alive. As the gate rolled up and the van moved out, I took a deep breath. It was like I was going home instead of to another prison. But I was leaving, and I was not leaving like I came twelve years ago; I was leaving with the right connection.

14

The Morning After

"If you can't do the time, don't do the crime."

Unknown

MOST PRISON POPULATIONS ARE divided in half, the inmates and the guards. Many inmates see these guards as the enemy, and many officers in turn view the inmates as animals. Because of the generalization on both parties, there is a great deal of friction, and the potential for violence is ever-present. The inmates make the mistake of holding the officers responsible for their imprisonment, and the officers err when they think their jobs consists of just turning keys. Both sides blunder when they fail to see each other as human beings, and both sides are guilty of misjudging when they allow uniforms and numbers to represent the enemy.

Society also errs when it permits the system to adopt a warehousing philosophy instead of a rehabilitative policy. Society makes the mistake when it fails to see the relation between itself and prisoners. What affects society also affects prisoners, whether it is positive or negative, good or bad.

Society makes the generalization that all prisoners are the same, but nothing is further from the truth. All inmates are not the same. Many inmates are in prison not as a result of committing crimes, but solely because of an economical system that allows 10% of the people to control 90% of its nation's wealth. Many are in prison because they could not afford high price attorneys to have their charges listed as embezzlement instead of grand theft. Many are in prison because they are innocent of all charges, but guilty of a greater crime of being born black and poor. Many are in prison because of a double standard justice system that demonstrates one set of laws for the wealthy and practices another set for the poor and underclass.

When white folks run the 100 yard dash, black folks have to run the 120 because we enter the race at a 20 yard disadvantage; we still have to be twice as good to get half as far. When white America is charged with drug abuse, it is a disease and they get treatment. But when blacks are charged with abusing drugs, it is a crime and they get prison, not treatment. Many are in prison because the system has exercised its choice of punishment where it attempts to "get blood out of a turnip" and condition prisoners to believe an institutional life is in their best interest, and is the only place they can survive. But most of all, society errs when it tries to understand prisoners through the eyes of the media.

When I arrived at the MHC, it was the same as any other prison. It was dirty, noisy, violent, and chaotic. It only had two cell blocks; the rest consisted of dorms, and they had trailers for the inmates with minimum status. At first I was housed in C-Dorm. It was for inmates who were idle or just arriving at the institution. The dorm was loud and noisy with over one hundred men. One of the first men I saw when I entered the dorm, was my old friend Floater. I spent most of my time with him. First he wanted to know how I was able to change my life, and when I told him my story he had nothing but words of encouragement; he was a wonderful friend. I tried to remind him that when he got tired help was available to him as well. Often people will not believe what you tell them, but they will believe what they see.

When I was able to move around the prison, I saw old friends and many familiar faces. Many had been here for years, but some had gone home only to return. The sad part, many if not most, were still beating their heads against a stone wall and playing a losing game.

Staying out of prison is a serious business. It is so serious that we, as prisoners, have not only failed—we have failed miserably. The recidivism rate is 74%; that means three out of every four inmates who leave prison will return. Those who return, why do they return so soon? Who is likely to succeed, and who is likely to fail?

It had been my experience to notice that there is a strong correlation between recidivism and education. Those who continue to return to prison have a limited education and see no advantage in its value. Behavioral psychologists probably suggest the cause is associated with inappropriate learning, whereby maladaptive behaviors are rewarded and adaptive behaviors are not. It is easy for an inmate to become conditioned to an institutional environment just as Pavlov's dogs became conditioned to the tone of the bell.

If the prisons were about the business of rehabilitation, they would strongly stress the importance of education, but too often they don't. In some prisons, officers have a negative attitude because the inmates are provided an opportunity to receive a college education.

"Why should they be allowed to get a free education, while my children have to pay a high cost?"

Well, that seems to be a legitimate complaint, but I am sure any inmate would gladly trade places with their children.

I began to take a Bible study course from Chaplain Gene Brown. He had a prison ministry in Delaware but later moved to Salisbury. He visited me often and we formed a beautiful and lasting relationship. I began to see the lack of education as another form of modem slavery, so I enrolled in school that June. After taking a diagnostic test, I was placed in school on a pre-GED level.

When I entered my English class, there was an extremely attractive young lady sitting behind a desk. She was stunningly beautiful and looked out of place in a prison setting. When the class began, she introduced herself as Ladell Johnson, and she was an excellent teacher. She taught at a fast level and gave plenty of homework each night. I stayed up every night studying when the lights went out because this was new to me, and I didn't want to get left behind. If you didn't study it was easy to get left behind, or sit in class looking stupid. In August I advanced to the GED Level, and I was in preparation to take the test that December. Now I studied even harder because I was determined to get my diploma.

Floater was released in October, and I moved to J-Dorm the following day. J-Dorm was made similar to C-Dorm, but it was larger and cleaner. However, we were still packed together like sardines in a can. As a result of overcrowding and other conditions, there was frequent violence. It was common to see an inmate charging down the aisle with his head bleeding like a pig, and when the lights went out you heard loud screams from men who had been scorched with boiling water. In a wide open dorm, if you had enemies, you were also at risk of being stabbed to death while you slept.

There is a certain population that has almost become extinct in prison; that population is the middle age prisoners. Today, prisoners are either young or old. Being housed in the dorm, I saw young inmates in the mirror for hours grooming themselves and flexing their muscles. Today, if you are over the age of 45, you are considered an old man. These men rarely used mirrors even to shave or comb their hair. They were afraid to see how old the image in the mirror had grown and they had no desire to be reminded of the truthfulness of their own appearance. As the prison population ages, the state will also have to pay a higher cost on this population's medical care; it is said one-third of the resources will be spent on the care of these inmates.

When I took the test in December, the results came back in three weeks and I had passed. I invited mom to my graduation because you could only invite one guest, and she was beaming with pride. Ms. Johnson encouraged us to continue our education, so I enrolled in Essex Community College that January. Taking five classes a semester, time passed swiftly, and there didn't seem to be enough hours in a day.

I had learned to make time serve me. Everything I could do to grow mentally and spiritually, I did it. I attended the Prison Fellowship seminar. I attended the concerts and revivals as well as went to church on Saturdays and Sundays. In addition to these activities, I got a job in the academy school as a teacher's aide in English.

In many ways I saw how modem conveniences came to disunite and isolate us, not only in prison but society as well. When we were permitted televisions and telephones, our reading decreased and the frequency of our written communication declined. Now televisions and telephones occupied a great portion of our time and we no longer had the time to read. Even the petitions that prisoners filed in the courts seeking legal redress diminished.

In society, the VCRs and microwaves and many other modem conveniences served to isolate families instead of bringing them closer together. Parents and children now ate meals in separate rooms, isolated from one another; no one ate as a family unit anymore. Now we had VCRs in every room, and each family member had the liberty of watching the show of his or her preference as they all grew further apart.

I had come so far so fast until I thought nothing could shake my foundation. But every now and then, even into a Christian life, trouble is going to knock at your door. No matter how strong you think you are in the faith, no matter how close you think you stand to God, and no matter how self-righteous you think you are in your own eyes, one day trouble is going to knock at your door and pay you a visit. When our faith is tested, then we see how strong we are and how close we stand to GOD. The soft winds had been blowing, but little did I know that just around the bend in the road, a mighty storm was brewing.

Early one morning a friend was telling me about a shooting he had heard in the District that night. He really knocked the wind out of me when he told me the victim who was shot nine times had the same first and last name as mine. Instantly, I knew it was my son; I could feel it deep in my soul. Minutes later when I called my sister, she confirmed it.

The papers reported it was drug related; he was suspected of being a major dealer and enforcer with a notorious organization operating within the city. Now I had to face the possibility that I would never see him again. Softy was gone; could I stand to lose him also?

It was one week before Thanksgiving and every day I called home to learn that he was doing better. Somehow I was sure everything was going to be all right. That dark cloud had vanished and so had my fears. A week later he was back home.

In March of *88 I wrote and designed an anti-drug pamphlet titled, *Marching to a Grave Song*, and I sent a copy to Pastor Durant. She worked with her production staff and put music to it and later put it on tape and narrated it on the air. I began to receive mail expressing how many lives had been touched by it, and I was encouraged to hold on and keep the faith. I needed to hear those words because in a few days the rain would fall again in my life, and I would feel the chill of the cold north wind. Several days later I called Daisy, but she nor mom was at home. Her girlfriend and next door neighbor answered the phone, and told me they were in church. Well, that wasn't unusual; they were always in church, so I talked to her for a while. She had been to visit me, and I considered her a friend with a good sense of humor. We were still laughing and talking when they came in.

"Hi sugar," I heard the voice of my sister.

"Hi baby; what was going on in church tonight?" I wanted to know.

"We weren't in church. We had to go to a wake."

"A wake!" I was trying to figure out who had passed away; what friend had died now!

"Didn't you get my letter?"

"Not yet."

There was a slight pause, and the rain fell. I heard the sound of thunder, and I felt the mighty winds blow into my life again.

"It was Jean's wake," I thought I heard her say. "Her funeral is tomorrow."

Why had I suddenly gone deaf? Why couldn't I make sense out of her words? When I finally made the connection, the earth shook beneath my feet, and I lost my voice and couldn't get my breath.

NO! Not my Jean! It couldn't be true; she couldn't be dead. Needing her was suddenly a part of me, and wanting her was a part of that need, but loving her was now all of me. The love of my life and the mother of my only children just couldn't be dead.

"...but it is going to be all right," my sister's voice came back to me.

When night came, I lay awake thinking of that special thing that we once had. On one hand we had given all we had. My pillow was wet with tears, and her memories were fresh in my heart, and her picture was a constant vision before me.

I thought about our lives together that night. I thought about what should have been, and could have been, but now it was much too late. Tonight, her sweet memories were all I had to warm my lonely soul. Jean—her sweet name I called again and again. My Jean! Forever the girl of my heart, you, my darling, will forever bum in the secret place of my soul.

Good-bye Jean; good-bye my love. I dried my eyes, and said good-bye to all my yesterdays. How I wish she could have lived long enough to see what God had done for me. I heard a voice speak to me in that moment, "My grace is sufficient for thee."

My son had been in Lorton only weeks. He had been charged with two first-degree murder charges and conspiracy to distribute cocaine and other crimes. However, I found the darkest hour is just before dawn, and the songbird sings the sweetest when the hour is the darkest. With these thoughts in my mind I began to write him.

Dear Son,

First, I thank God every day for you, and I greet you this day with the love of a father, friend, and companion.

You were our firstborn, and you brought so much joy and happiness into our world and life. Oh, how proud your mother and I were when we found out she was with child. You were our dreams; you were our life. You were a symbol of courage, hope, and a brighter day.

To us, you were like a little savior, and we looked for you to deliver us, somehow and some way, from the dregs and worthless and useless parts of life that enslaved us and held us captive against our will.

So, you came, my son, into our steaming, mad world. You came wet, black, and screaming to make your own little presence known. And the world stood by and watched us with a wicked and deceitful smile as if it knew our future and fate.

The world laughed because it knew you had to stand as a black man-child in the twenty-first century surrounded by drugs, fast money, glamour, plastic dreams and illusions. And it knew our deliverance was not to come. We had been programmed toward the pig trough, and the odds were stacked against us that we would never get out of the rut.

Deliver us, son! Deliver us; we cried!

But we were already programmed for life. We were trapped in a world that always cried more. No matter how much we fed it, it continued to cry, feed me! Feed me—and feed it we did.

We gave it our youth, our laughter, our tears, and our blood. But oh—look what it gave us in return. It gave us fresh-marked graves, heartaches, and tears. It gave us broken lives, broken promises, and broken dreams. It gave us lies, bad times, and the blues. It gave us promises of fame and riches, but in return it gave us padded rooms in the insane asylums. On one hand it gave us too little, but on the other hand it took way too much.

It gave us too much pain, too much confusion, madness, danger, trouble, and grief. The best it could give us if we were lucky was prison.

Here we were forced to be still long enough to listen to the inner voice speak and reveal to us the truth. It let us know that the world was a lie, and it had influenced us to take part in a game that was impossible for us to win. It gave us a new lease on life and a second chance.

So where do we go from here, my son?

We must take advantage of it. If not, we will continue to fail, and make the same old mistakes over and over again.

But 1 want you to always know and remember, my son, I am just as proud of you today, as I was when I first learned of your conception.

Love,
Your father Cheese

Rev. Charlotte Sims was one of the many who began to correspond with me since she heard my song on the radio. After months of corresponding, I received her permission to put her name on my visiting list. Two days later she sent me three additional names: Rev. E. Pressley and his wife W. Pressley, Sis. Dorothy Gray, and later Sis. D. Wilson. Rev. Sims was also a school teacher and would work with me closely in getting my manuscript published. Also Sisters Pressley and Gray would type it when it was completed.

When I first met Rev. Sims, I was completely surprised. Somehow I had a preconceived idea in my head what she would be like, but I was wrong in every way. She was young, attractive, and possessed a sweet spirit and kind soul. But her best quality was her level of spirituality; that stood out above all others. Mostly they came as a group, and they became like a part of my family. Later, other inmates joined our fellowship, and we grew in number. Sometimes Rev. Sims came alone; those visits I really treasured, and we saw our relationship grow with each passing day.

Rev. John E. Wormley, our family pastor and founder of Kingdom of Zion Baptist Church, kept me encouraged with his communication and prayers. Many inmates made the tragic mistake of re-establishing relationships with former acquaintances. But when you change your old habits, you must also change your friends. Slowly I found myself being surrounded by new friends that sincerely loved me with my family, and they wanted to see my new life continue in the direction it was going.

Life has taught me many important and valuable lessons. I came to the realization one day that I've always been my greatest enemy. It was the enemy who made me blame others for my mistakes and bad choices. It was the enemy who made me look outward instead of inward. It was the enemy who made me focus on the results and not the cause. It was the enemy who made me hate others so much until I hated myself the most.

It was not until I was able to kill the enemy within that I was totally set free. When the enemy died, it was no longer necessary to play games and there was no need to continue the masquerade. I could be myself and be proud of who I was. I've learned that my weakness was the mask and being myself was my greatest strength and access.

"If you can't do the time, don't do the crime." Those who are guilty of committing crimes are those who complain the most and cry the loudest. But I have learned from first-hand experience that "crime doesn't pay," especially if you are a member of the underclass, for the underclass will always have to fight for a voice in a system that has no intention of treating them as equals.

Make no mistake about it, prison life is hell. Nevertheless, experience has taught me that even in the darkest of night there is a ray of light. In other words, there are very few things that I consider 100% all bad, even prison.

If we tell the complete story, then we must admit prison has saved a multitude of lives. Many men who were caught up in drugs and a violent lifestyle would have perished if they were allowed to continue their course of action without a temporary interruption.

Although my chronological age was 29 when I entered prison, I matured from a boy to a man; that is not the norm in prison, but an exception. Usually, prison makes boys, not men. Men are responsible;

boys are irresponsible. Men elevate their women; boys debase them in the name of deception and false love. Men see an obstacle as a challenge; boys see it as a stumbling block. Men take the advantage of today; boys delay things until a later date, however, seldom is anything accomplished. Men have visions of the future; boys have stale dreams of the past. Men have priorities; boys take life as it comes.

There is a pendulum swinging in the life of every individual who enters prison, and he alone must decide if he will become a boy or man. He must decide if he will take the worst the system has to offer and use it in a beneficial or destructive manner. I believe everyone deserves a chance to redeem himself, and those who are provided an opportunity must make the best out of it.

On August 25, 1988, I graduated from Essex Community College. My mother, sister, and Olivia attended my graduation ceremony. Olivia was my sister's girlfriend, and she often came to visit me with them. I thought back to June of 1'86 when I only had a tenth grade education, but now I was standing on stage dressed in a cap and gown with a degree in my hand.

There I stood with thoughts of Jean, Chester, Softy, Fly, Ann, and Cindy heavy on my mind, if they were only here to see me now. Look—look what God had done for me. I thought about all my friends who had lived and died in prison in hopelessness and despair. I thought about so many who had died without knowing, regardless of their crimes or sins, SOMEONE forgives, SOMEONE loves, and SOMEONE cares. Some of these men had died from a plain old broken heart; they were poor souls who had given up on life, believing they were unloved and unwanted.

Today, I am a senior at Coppin State College majoring in psychology, working toward my bachelor's degree. I don't know what tomorrow will bring, and I am not sure when the winds will blow into my life again, but I have SOMEONE who will make the difference between victory and defeat, and life and death. His voice is a constant whisper in my ears, "My grace is sufficient for thee."

I had died for the last time when I accepted Him in faith, and my family and I had finally found our long lost PROMISED LAND.

15

The Long Ride Back

PRISON IS THE NAME GIVEN TO A PLACE CALL HELL, WHERE MANY SOULS SUFFER IN AGONY DAILY UNDER THE VICIOUS SYSTEM OF... JUSTICE.

HUEY P. NEWTON

ONCE AGAIN, I SAT gazing out at the REAL WORLD' that lie just beyond tall fences and sharp razor wire. This is my world, the only one I have known over the past 20 years, and I don't know if I have another one left in me. It IS a lonely and oftentimes violent world, a world in which I have come to know so well.

It is a living hell that knows no mercy. It is a million dreams that can never be fulfilled. It is too many tears without laughter, too much darkness without light. IT is a world where we wake up every morning with the same old fears, same old loneliness, same old depression, and the same old physical ailments.

One of the hardest things about coming to prison is giving up our rights as free men. The right to make decisions about food, clothes, privacy, are all gone; so we are inclined to fight against the system for denying us these rights.

But this is my world, where no person should want to come, but we do, not once, but again and again we return; and this is something not fully understood, a mystery. Could there be a correlation between classical conditioning and our return to prison like Pavlov/s dog begin to salivate at the sound of a bell? How can it be explained or made clear?

Nevertheless, welcome to my world, a hell like no other. It sinks its teeth into the human flesh just like a dog with a rag doll. It crushes you from the inside out leaving you in a state of depression and hopelessness. It affects every aspect of human existence, spiritually, mentally, and physically. It literally beats you down making you feel that life is not worth living, and there is no way to escape from its grip.

One second, the sun is shining bright, but the next heartbeat, it's totally darkness and despair. It will try to convince you that you are worthless, and you're a walking dead man looking for a place to fall and you will never leave this place alive again to live in a world without walls. Yet, in the face of overwhelming odds, you must cast aside these beliefs, and believe there is a better day, even for you.

It will not be easy, and it will take all of your effort to succeed. Some way you must rise from your ashes like a mythological sphinx with the words "it is not over until the fat lady sings", but better still, with these words, "it's not over until God says its over", because He still has a plan for our lives. There will be critics and haters; that's a part of life, and they will still be criticizing and hating us on our way to our destiny.

As I continued to gaze out at the "real world" I am confronted with the reality of death and dying in prison. In the coming years, I would have to deal with death in an unfamiliar way. But this time it would not be my demise, but the passing of those whom I have loved the most in my life, bring me to the brink of madness, and for years to come, I would mourn their passing.

A.W. Tozer wrote, "We poor human creatures are constantly being frustrated by the limitations imposed on us. The days of the years of our lives are short. Life is a short and fevered rehearsal for a concert we cannot stay to give. Just when we appear to have gained some proficiency, we are forced to lay our instruments down."

Today turned out to be just another day in prison; nothing extraordinary, just another day. Usually we can tell what day it in by looking at the food on the menu. I stayed up late studying for my final exam, and then called it a night. Sometime before sunrise, there was a loud commotion in the back of the dormitory where I was housed with more than one hundred other inmates. Suddenly the large dorm was in an uproar. A small group of men were chasing another inmate between the narrow passage of beds. His upper body was covered with Blood, and he began to leap over bunk after bunk as he tried to make it to the front where the officer was stationed.

Before he could reach the front, he tripped and fell to the floor, and was douched with a flammable liquid and set on fire, and his body quickly became an inferno. He made a loud piercing sound like an animal caught in a snare. He struggled to save his life, and no one would dare render aid. A large number of officers rushed in and apprehend the guilty parties. The hospital staff was called, and he was rushed out to a local hospital, but his face and upper torso were scared for life, leaving him disfigured, but no one would dare identify his true assailants.

When we have a disagreement or a beef in prison, we don't seek a peaceful resolution; that would be too civilized and contrary to the prison code. Our reputation and status is always at stake, so we don't look for a solution, we rather maim or go for the jugular.

One day when I looked at the calendar, the year was 1992, and I begin for the first time to think about freedom and a life beyond my present condition. It is one of those illusive terms that doesn't mean the same for everyone. It is one of those incomparable entitlements we enjoy as citizens in America. However, there is a point in time when that right becomes void, and that liberty is waived. For example, if you are convicted of a crime against a person or the state, that privilege is no longer in effect.

Everyone has the freedom of choice, and the minute we make any choice, we set into motion consequences that will be consistent with our choices; and once they are made, the outcome is no longer in our hands. I made a terrible bad choice in 1973, one of which I wish I could take back but, can't, and I would spend 40 years fighting in the belly of a vicious beast consuming my flesh as a down payment for my choices and sins. In retrospect, if I had been aware of this knowledge, perhaps my life would have turned out much different, but somehow that doesn't matter now.

Each night I closed my eyes wishing to escape the pain of my reality, but every morning, it would only be a repeat of sorrow and sadness. My life has been written, debated, and seen in various moves, but nothing can accurately depict my life, unless it is unfortunately experienced. Regardless of one's status on the streets, it does not mean it will render the same once inside. When the steel gates slam shut with the sounds of an earthquake, there will be an element of fear of the unpredictable, and if you give in to it; it will conquer you, and you will become a person that you hate; but 1992 proved to be a good year for me.

I was approved to be transferred to camp, minimum security. Camp was the place offenders were transferred when their release date was approaching or soon anticipated. It was devised to slowly integrate inmates back into society with employment and resources that they would need to succeed and not return. It was a noble concept, but not too successful. For years the recidivism rate has been consistent between 60-70 percent. For every 4 that leaves, 3 return having committed more serious crimes and with longer sentences. Nevertheless, we have the power to change, but change means giving up our self-proclaimed power and live according to society's rules, but that is a price so many are unwilling to pay.

Hey Cheese", I heard someone calling my name.

When I turned to see who it was, it was Fat Hardy, one of my dearest friends. I heard "you were on your way out," he said. Most of my friends no longer identified me by my surname Cheese, and those who did, it was an indication we had a long history and friendship.

Each Night, I Die

I was beyond ecstatic to be leaving. I gave away most of my clothes, appliances, and toiletries. On the day of my departure I said goodbye with mixed emotions. We had all been together for so many years we were like family. We had hustled together, fought together, and even cried together over our losses; and here I was saying goodbye knowing I would never see many of them again in this life.

My few boxes were by the exit door when the transportation officer came to transport me. When he approached me, I extended my hands for him to put on the manacles; no one leaves the prison without restraints. What's that for, he asked? I was somewhat dumbfound, and he continued, Those days for you are over now, you can put your boxes in the van and get in.'

There were three other inmates in the van, and they too were going to camp. Jessup Maryland was a large complex with 6 other institutions, and it was a short ride from MCI, where I had spent the last 6 years to my destination JPRU.

When I first arrived, the atmosphere was totally different what I had experienced. This was the day I thought would never come, and a time I thought I would never live to see. But here I was with one foot in, and one foot out. I was so close to home I could almost smell it.

My friend, Charlotte, came to visit the following day. She and I were in a serious relationship, and we were making plans for my soon release. When I entered the room, she was all smiles, and I was welcomed with a warm hug and a short kiss, and then we took our seat at the table. The room had a soda and vending machines for refreshment. After a short time she asked, "Would you like some snacks?" *Sure*, was my response.

I walked with her to the area with the machines and stood by her side. She opened her purse and removed a handful of single bills. I was puzzled and mystified as I stood there having a conversation with myself. *What does she plan to do with those bills?* I thought to myself. I didn't have long to wait for my answer. One by one she placed a bill into a slot on the machine, and the bill slowly disappeared out of site into the machine.

WOW,'I exhaled, *They have machines now that take paper money*. That was the first time I had seen that, and I was flabbergasted to say the least. During my long prison term, these had to be among my better days. I was in constant communication with my publisher, Mike Duncan. Once I sent him my manuscript he said he was compelled to publish it because it had the potential to help so many other.

After approximately two week after I was there, my publisher, came to visit me, and to my surprise, he had copies of my just released book. It received national publicity, and three times a week I was giving radio interviews from coast to coast. Yes, these were my best days, but life has a way of presenting us with situations beyond our control, and so it was on the day of June 2, 1993.

I had been watching the NBA championship playoff and just fallen to sleep, when suddenly, Get up and get dressed', said one of the three officers surrounding my bed. The bright were on high, and I noticed officers standing at the beds of every lifer in the dorm.

'When you get dressed, remove all the money from your locker, and then lock it," was the order of another.

"But I never lock my locker" I said in a mild protest. I said, "get up and remove all the money from your locker, and then lock it," was the order, this time spoken more forceful. I obeyed, but couldn't comprehend what this was all about. When I was dressed, they put the cuffs on me, and I was marched outside where the local police had surrounded the entire camp.

Once inside the dining room, it was full of more security and armed transportation officers. Then it hit me. We were all being transferred back to medium security institutions were we had once been housed, all 60 of us, and there were 72 other that were at camp.

Rodney Stokes, a lifer who was on work release, killed his girlfriend and then committed suicide, and the results was 132 lifers being removed from the system, and to this day, never returned. Most of us had come through the trenched together and had to say goodbye to those who succumbed to the unexpected enemy of death, and soon, we would become members of a dying breed in prison. We boarded the three busses heavily shacked, and it would be a long trip to Hagerstown at 1am. It was a rainy night, which only added to our spirit of gloom. Suddenly I recalled what the officer had told me when I left that these days were now behind me. I'm sure it was an honest prediction, but none of us can predict the future, because most of us are too preoccupied with the here and now.

Each inmate was chained to another, and my partner was Greg, one of my close friends who would die in prison. Hagerstown was not new to him. He had been there at an earlier time when he was much younger.

Damn, I have to go back into these mountains and watch Dr. Who and 25 alive," but I had no idea what he was talking about, but soon it would become crystal clear. "Dr. Who," I asked?

You'll find out what it is in a minute," was his response. 25 alive was a local television program, and Dr. Who was a late night weekend program. During the long ride back, I felt the pulse of my peers and felt their gloom and despair. We had done no wrong, committed no offense; but we were being punished 134 men, for the offense of one individual. And now we were taking the long ride back to a place and time we thought we would never return. Life is not always fair, but this was beyond the scope of our comprehension.

The ride back would prove to be fatal for many. Some would give up their struggle for freedom and accept the ride as the final chapter in their long quest for freedom. Some would die from drugs, cancer, and a host of diseases that accompany old age, and I would have to lock myself into my own private world and weep for so many lives gone too soon.

I once believed we lived in a world that believed in second chances, no matter what the offense. If we change our lives, play by the rules and do the right thing, there should be some tangible or intangible reward at the end. We have the privilege of living in the greatest country on the planet, but it is not always right, and there will always be people who will hold it against us, not because of who we are, but simply because of where we have been. No matter what noble or good we contributed, their position would never change.

Upon our arrival the officials didn't know how we would react to our situation. Would we initiate some form of violence? Would we embark upon rioting or create turmoil? They just didn't know what our reaction would be. But our response was consistent with the men we had grown to become. If it had been otherwise, it would have validated their position and weaken ours. I sensed also there were many inmates who were sure our reaction would end in some major disturbance, but they too were wrong. All that we wanted to do was to return home and live a simple life.

I was not surprised to see so many old and familiar faces, but I was surprised, to see how much it had changed in so short of time. Prison gangs had emerged and they waged war over who had the right to occupy certain prison turf as it was their own personal territory.

Nevertheless, make no misstate about it, prison was still prison, an unnatural environment, and I concur with an unknown writer's views who wrote about prison and said:

Prison is a loneliness and sinks its teeth into the very soul of men. It is overlooked, and unrecorded by newspapers, seldom read of in any books, and rarely portrayed on the screen; its a place where people starve to find themselves.

It is a place of both hope and hopelessness, Its dreams that can never be fulfilled. It is too many tears without laughter, too much emotional darkness without light. It is routine that makes living a weary task.

It is the bitterness of those without friends. It is the unhappiness of an undisciplined life. Where discipline is neglected, life wanders into habits, habits into bondage and things that dictate life's direction. It is a worried mother's face studying the face of a son who was once her pride and joy. Her heart is now broken because drugs are destroying him, and there is nothing that she can do about it.

For years I tried to outrun life, but in every attempt it only ended in failure. How could I outrun my past when it has proven to be a tenacious and insidious creature? Things I once cherished became less frequent, and then all but forgotten. I believe life will one day brings us to a crossroad where we are forced to examine our lives, and where we ask ourselves the critical question concerning it. Why am I here? What is my purpose?

On both sides of the fence the question will be the same, is this all that life has to offer? If it is, we will find it hard to go on living. When we come to the crossroad, we must look long and hard into the mirror and see beyond the superficial and see what's authentic and what's worth fighting for; and living for. When we see the worst part in us, we must be willing to kill it, so that the best part can thrive and grow.

When one gives an account of prison, the narrative is usually described in two words, a living hell'. However, that analogy can be deceiving, and it does not tell the whole story. During the course of my life, I have discovered even at our lowest and hardest times, we can find some good. Therefore, prison can be exactly what we make.

I have literally witness some men find themselves and their passion while in prison. Malcolm X did it; Nelson Mandela did it; Charles "Rock' Dutton did it, and so it is today, in the twenty first century, men are continuing to find themselves and their passion in prison. The number may not be impressive, but some have found their heaven in the midst of their hell. Our worst times does not have to define us. Also, hell is not necessarily confined behind the walls. Every morning the sun rise above the urban streets of the cities, and millions rise early in the morning to go on jobs not because they love then, but because of the necessity to put food on the table to feed their families, and at some point they will struggle with the same issues we do in prison, and the struggles they encounter can turn their world upside down and become a living hell.

The winter sun still rise and set above the dirty city streets. The strong still exercise their position and influence to benefit themselves at the expense of the poor. Many men and women walk the city streets, who have become mentally deranged, begging for a few coins from pedestrians because they are locked out of a system and left to fend for themselves. Too many politicians become corrupt and unethical. Too many clergymen refuse to practice what they preach and they become rich in promises, but poor in blessings.

Lonely souls who have no hope stare out on the city streets. They are mourners and soft singers of funeral hymns for those who die from neglect, pressure, and violence. They are mothers and sisters mourning for husbands and fathers MIA (missing in action). They have seen us come within inches of our best dreams, artificial dreams that never were.

YES, America, is still ripe with mourners, hymns, and artificial dreams in the twenty first century, and hell can never be designated to a particular geographical location.

Today, I sat all alone in the rear of a dimly lighted restaurant, loss in my private thoughts; thoughts concerning a beautiful woman, love, and me. Then I see her, and she is absolutely gorgeous, and her beauty is beyond description.

She entered the room with an air of confidence like a beauty queen on a runway platform. I hear her speak, and it is the soulful voice of an angel, and it is recognizable among the voices of millions. When she strolled into the restaurant, her sweet fragrance dominated the atmosphere with the scent of misty blue.

I am captured by her elegance and splendor. I asked myself, "who is this woman, and where did she come from?' If I attempted to describe her imagery, it would only mar and cloud the picture. She takes a seat diagonally from the table I am seated. She gently holds the menu in her left hand while the other rested on her delicate chin. Without warning she glance in my direction, and our eyes locked for a second in time, and she looks again at her menu with a faint smile on her delicate lips.

Should I continue to admire her at a distant? What should I do? If I approached her, would she interpret it as being rude or insensitive? For a few short minutes I pondered my dilemma, and I was determined not to let it slip away. In the twinkling of an eye, I rose from the table making my way in her direction. A few paces from her table, suddenly there was a loud sounding bell announcing it was count time, the most important time in prison where everyone must be accounted for. Immediately, I snapped out of it realizing it was only my imagination, a common occurrence for men in prison.

> WHEN SOMEONE IS IN A STORM, THEY DON'T NEED SOMEONE TO TALK OR TELL THEM ABOUT THE WEATHER; THEY NEED SOME ONE TO HOLD ON TO

Somehow I have always been my own worst enemy. I thought the worst days of my life was over, but tomorrow brings its own problems that can't be anticipated or predicted. I had envisioned the "the morning after" to be a time exempted from struggles, but life render no such promise or guarantee. Regardless of one's status in life, we all encounter disappointments, pain, loss, and suffering. If we only had the ability to see into the future, we could be prepared for those crisis situations.

One week after we arrived, I received my bachelor's degree from Coppin State with a concentration in addiction counseling. I had heard that good things rarely come in twos, but trouble never walks alone. My son who was now 19 had been charged with two counts of murder and drug distribution. He had become a major player in the drug trade that was causing widespread destruction and violence on the urban streets of Washington. At his trial, a jury found him not guilty of the murders, but guilty of drug distribution, and he was sentenced to 30 years in the federal penitentiary.

John Wildeman once wrote: "Prison depends on make believe the sign above the prison entrance doesn't read Abandon Hope; it says Abandon Yourself, while he was in prison, I tried to write him every single day. I wanted him to know I was no longer THAT MAN' that he thought I was; that person died in 1983; as a result, my life had been completely transformed. In every one of my letters this is the message I tried to communicate, but somewhere deep within me, I knew I was fighting an uphill battle. To him, my story was too good to be true, and nothing I wrote could erase the image of me that was seared in the conscious of his tender mind, the image of a thug father and drug dealer.

Every child deserves the right to have their fathers physically presence, but selfish and illicit choices deny them that right. Approximately 5 years later, he was released from prison. I wanted him to understand he had been given another chance, and that his life didn't have to be a parallel to mine, but again, I knew it was too late for such a conversation because the die had been cast while he was still in the cradle, and my bad choices didn't give him much of a chance.

I wonder how many fathers will now have the courage to reach out to their wayward sons before it's too late? How many fathers will now break the vicious cycle once and for all like father, like son? Too many of our sons are dying young, dying early, dying of drugs, dying of violence, and dying repeating the identical choices of their fathers. The strength of a nation is seen and measured by its men, but too often sons look for their fathers, and we become like Casper the Ghost.

Thinking about his young life, my mind and thoughts returned to that day when I first saw him lying in his mother's arms as I looked at him through a small Plexiglas window at the DC jail. In his book, THE MAN IN THE MIRROR, Patrick Morley talks about the story of the wicked witch in Snow White. "The witch was obsessed with the desire to be the most beautiful woman in the land. She loved the mirror so much she spoke to it with terms of endearment, until one day the mirror gave her an answer she didn't know which she hated more, Snow White or the mirror that refused to lie"

I desperately tried to get my son to look at that man in the mirror, but all he could still see was the image of his father's life. In the spring of 1994, I was summoned to the chaplain office, but this was not unusual. Frequently I was asked to perform some duty for the congregation. But on my way there, I suddenly had an uneasy feeling about this trip; then it hit me, this was about "death', this was about someone's demise, but who could it be this time?

When I arrived at here office, Chaplain Day and I had a brief discussion about my son. Then with much empathy, she told me that my son had been shot. HE DIED TWO DAYS BEFORE HIS 24th birthday.

'NO', I scream, "NO, NO, he can't be dead" I sat there weeping with my head buried in my hands, and I thought about the last words he said to me!' Daddy, all of my life, I wanted to be just like you"

Like me, like me! "NO, not like me, my son. You can be better, do better! But his haunting words would ring in my ears as long as I live. If my way of life wasn't good for him, then why was it so good for me. Many years ago, these were the same words my brother had asked me, and I had no answer for him then, and I had no answer for my son now.

Contemplating his young life, my thoughts raced back to the very first time I saw him lying in his mother's arms as I looked at him through a small Plexiglas window at the DC Jail. No other time in my life could I ever recall being more happy than I was that day; and now, no other event in life could make me more sadder than I was at that very moment, and my heart broke into a thousand shattered pieces, for a son gone too soon from his father.

This was the day in my life when I should have rose from the table, cashed in my chips, and walked away from the game, once and for all. I should have told myself, "Look at him, look at him; he is your son, and it cannot be all about you anymore. What you do from this point on will not only affect you, but also impact his life as well. This is the conversation I should have had with myself. Now, it's too late for him and much too late for me, because sometimes life events does not offer us a second chance. Now, his body rest in a grave in the cold bosom of the earth in Lincoln Cemetery along with his mother, what a tragedy; both leaving my life and the world much too soon.

Inside the fence I observed the rapid decline of our once powerful social institutions, and as they go, so goes the lives of our people, particular our children. We have become in essence a violent prone society, and we feed our children with an unhealthy diet of violence and aggression, and conflict resolution, has in effect become a thing of the past. When our children have a disagreement, they no longer talk it out, they take it to the matt, with aggression and violence, a learned reaction.

If we, as parents, want our children to be better, we must ourselves become better. To say to our children "don't do as I do; do as I say, may have a good sounding effect, but it never has been a real solution, and I have learned nothing our youngsters hate more than hypocrisy.

When I left the chaplains office, I had no knowledge how long it took me to arrive back to my cell. I staggered back in a daze, disorient, and discombobulated. I had lost all sense of time and space. My feelings were numb and dead, and the only comfort I had at the time was my numbness. With every step that I took, I recall saying over and over again "Lord, don't let me fall apart out here."

My friends and peers seemed to know what had occurred. No one had to tell them, it was seen on my face. When the cell door closed, everything inside of me erupted and I fell to the floor beside my bunk sobbing, incoherently,

"My son, my son, why did you have to leave your father so soon. There is so much I wanted to tell you. I wanted to tell you how much I really loved you. You were my world, my life, my everything. Did you know my son, that you possessed the power to turn my worst day into the best." But now he's gone, and he will never hear what I had to say to him. Every so often, one of my friends would come to the door and attempt to comfort me. But at the time, there could be no solace or comfort for me. That would take years to come, and even today there are times when I struggle with his loss.

No one can frilly understand what it is like for a parent to lose a child unless they have experienced the lost themselves. The only positive thing that I could take from this experience was I still had one child left, my daughter, Vickie.

When we come to prison, we lose our identities, our relationships, and much, much more. It is the height of insanity when we look at the tradeoff we make for the dull routine life in prison, and sometimes, yes sometimes, we even lose our children.

I wish I had been a better father. I loved him so much, yet my love for him was not strong enough to make me change my life for the better, and to this very day I have to live with the agonizing pain that I was complacent, in many ways, to in his early death.

I recall when he was only two years old my mother said to me one day.

"Boy," yes, that's how mothers talked back then; "If you ever do anything that will cause you to be separated from him, you are going to pay a heavy price because you love him too much." How does mothers always seem know about things we are unaware of and unable to see?

I once recall a writer who had a profound love for plants. As a matter of fact, he thought flowers were the most attractive and ravishing sight on earth. Although he had an immense love for flowers, he didn't know how to care for them, or what it took to make them grow, or what it took to prevent blight and to keep them healthy, and free from diseases. Therefore, one could deduce or surmise, this writer had a brainless love for flowers, as some people have a brainless love for their children. Their love for their children can never be called into question, but the question at issue becomes what is their method of parenting.

The love I had for my son was never in question, but I didn't know what it took to be a father; therefore, I also had a brainless love for my son. For example, I could never recall disciplining him, but now I know that love without discipline is no love at all. No guide has ever been written on how to raise perfect children, perhaps good, but not perfect, simply because perfection is not a characteristic of human nature, and bring up children in today's world has to be the most difficult task on the planet.

I was sitting alone in deep thought as I was reading a book when one of my peers by the name of Sammy entered my space. I laid my book next to me on my bed and asked, "What's up?"

"Cheese, there is something I have to tell you that I am sure you don't know."

"How many years have you known me, Sammy? Then you know there is not much that I don't know these days. With people talking so much and telling so many lies, there are very few things in prison that are still concealed. So again, what's up, man?"

"I'm going to give it to you raw, straight, no chaser. One of your main men is using again."

"Who are you talking about? Put a name to who you are talking about if you don't want him to remain anonymous."

"It's Fat Man."

It took me a minute to recover. He was talking about a man who stood as close to me as a heartbeat. Our lives were once consumed with drugs, jump steady, and hustling, but we both had gone through a transformation, and our lives had been changed, and now I am hearing he is using again, get out of here!

"Man, when will you jokers stop spreading gossip and innuendos on other people? And before you get out of my space, I want you to know, you're throwing dirty on a good man."

"I am not telling you second hand information, I am only telling you what I've seen with my own eyes, and the only reason I am bring it to you, because of all people you may be the only one who can help him now."

When he left, I had to digest what he had said. I could see in the dark, and I could walk across a desert and leave no footprints in the sand. The signs he was using were visible, but I refused to accept he had returned to what we both had been delivered from, years of addiction and iniquity. He had played a major role in my metamorphose, and now I had to confront him. I had to confront him because he was my friend.

When I saw him, he was with a small group of "the boys" who were players in the game, another tail sign of his relapse. "Fat man," I called him to the side for a private conversation.

"What's up bro? I know you are using again, and I have to say something to you because you know I love you, and you are one of my closest friends!"

He spoke no words, and he just looked at me with the eyes of shame and humiliation. We talked for more than an hour. He tried to analyze his relapse. I was not there to humiliate him, I just wanted him to know I was there for him, as he was once for me. As we talked, I understood him, but because I was his friend, I could never sanction what he was doing.

The noted author James Baldwin wrote:

Every... boy... realize, at once, profoundly, because he wants to live, that he stands in great peril and must find, with speed, a thing, a gimmick, to lift him out to start him on his way. And it does not matter what the gimmick is.

I understood my friend. I knew exactly where he was, and that's why I had to confront him. It is better to win an enemy by speaking the truth, than to win a friend by flattery. No one can predict how one's story or life will end. And certainly I would never be able to forecast the final chapter in his journey, but that would be years to come.

Several weeks before we were checked in from camp in 1993, I was taking my noon day nap when I was awaken by an officer announcing:

"Cheese, get up. The commissioner is here to see you."

There was an urgency in his voice and tone I didn't understand. Who was the commissioner, and why did he want to see me? I carefully reviewed my recent activities to see if I had committed a violation or infringement, but there was none. Since 1985, my life had been untainted.

The officer escorted me to the unit manager's office, and there I was introduced to the Commissioner of Correction, Richard A. Lanham, Sr. As soon as I saw him, I knew he was a person of significance and prestige.

"Hello Cheese," he said as he extended his hand. "I am Commissioner Lanham, I just completed reading your book. It is an amazing book, and it should be read by everyone."

We talked for approximately 45 minutes on a variety of issues, and that day was the beginning of a long and personal relationship, and he became one of my most vigorous and vibrant supporters. He communicated to the warden my involvement with the youth, and one night I received a pass to attend one of the prison's self-help organizations, Lifestyles.

The organization consist of six subcommittees, one of which was Prisoners Against Teen Tragedy (PATT), a youth diversion and community education program, and for more than 20 years I had the privilege to be its director. It was here I found my passion and calling in life, along with my leadership role in the nondenominational church.

In PATT we target at risk youth who were most vulnerable to negative peer pressure, and we believe all youth are "at risk", simply because none of them are exempt from the everyday influences they encounter on a daily basic.

As we share our stories and have meaningful dialogue, they are able to see positive choices yield positive results, while negative choices give birth to oftentimes tragic consequences; and this is critical because too often they fail make a connection between their choices and their consequences. And whenever one choose to break the law or commit a crime, he or she must be willing to accept everything that goes along with it, including prison; and that's one thing we lay it all on the line to keep them from experiencing.

I vividly recall my first experience. It was with one of Maryland's juvenile facilities with some youth convicted for crimes as serious as murder. After they are taken on a physical tour of the prison where they see and hear for themselves the unpleasant sights and sounds that are in themselves frighten and appalling.

When they enter the room, we state our numbers, sentences, and years of incarceration; our names are unimportant; we left them at the gate, and now we are known as a six digit number, and then they hear our stories.

"My name is m-050, and I am doing life, and I have been here longer before any of you were born. How did I get here? The same way most of you got where you are today. I didn't know how to deal with negative peer pressure, so I conformed to the expectation of my so-called friends. Whatever they did I did also because I wanted to fit in, no matter what. One day I went along with three of them to buy beer, and two of them I knew were committing crimes, but I went along anyway. Two of them entered the store, and after several minutes, I hear this loud explosive sound BAND! They ran out of the store, jumped into the car, "let's go, let's go" they shouted. Unbeknown to me they went there with the intent of robbing the store, but in the process, they also committed murder. Don't let my story become your story."

The next member went on to talk about drugs. Prisons today are full of inmates who got involved with drugs. At first it was just for fun: a little weed, a little meth, a little heroin, a little crack, and suddenly their fun is turned into a nightmare, as their lives are completely destroyed.

The next one talked about the importance of education. Malcolm X wrote: "Education is our passport to the future, for tomorrow belongs to those who prepare for it today." Education transcend academic knowledge. It is the knowledge learned in the classroom and applied to everyday life and survival.

In her book, A SIN AGAINST THE FUTURE, Vivien Stern asked a warden of a large prison to describe his worst problem. His answer was not what she had expected. He said most men read at a third grade level or below, and 2/3 will return to prison. How much money, he asked, did congress set aside for literacy programs? Not one dime!

We also talk to young females because girls under the age of 18 have become the fastest growing segment in the juvenile justice system, and they are often placed in setting and institutions that are neither designed for nor proven effective in their treatment and rehabilitation.

The most reliable predictor of a child going to prison is that his mother or father is already there, and 1 of 14 African American children has a parent in prison. We talk about all of the issues that are critical for them to make good choices.

I believe our program is the best in the nation because of our motto: Because we care and our ability to listen. We cannot be absorbed in ourselves, and listening takes time, energy, and lots of patience. We try to listen with our eyes, seeing their pain, fears, or joy. What makes us different is we listen with our heart, seeing how important they are to us. Mostly important, we try to listen with our spirit. This validates them as a person, and oftentimes it does not require a solution response.

I have talked to over 10,000 young boys and girls, and as I have stood before them I have seen in their faces, the face of my son. I couldn't reach him, but I can be a positive influence on them and motivate them to do better, be better, because their lives really are in their hands, and only they can determine what it will be.

In his book THE INCREDIBLE POWER OF GRACE, Ronald R. Hegstad wrote:

> Call a chair ugly, and nothing happens to it. He says even if it's a Chippendale, it just sits there, neither insulted nor embarrassed. But call a child ugly or stupid or clumsy often enough and he will become to believe it. Stamped on the mental map of a tender person is the conviction that he is stupid. He gives up on himself believing that safety lies in not trying. His life motto becomes "If I don't try, I can't fail.

I often think about the countless youth I've talked with, all of the ones in juvenile facilities, all of the young men currently in prison today, and I wonder how many of them are locked away because one day they were told they were ugly, stupid, or a loser? I think about all of the children whose dreams have died as a result to self-fulfilling prophecies.

No child should ever have to hear these words spoken to them, or about them, especially not from a parent or a guardian. We are the gatekeepers of our children and we are given the charge to persuade, inspire, and give them the confidence they need to achieve their dreams and obtain their goals.

We believe our program featured on episode 5 Beyond Straight, is the best in the nation, and we close our session with a poem written by an ex offender that is titled:

WASTED TIME

The time that I've wasted is my biggest regret, spent in these places I
will never forget.
Just sitting and thinking I've done.
The crying, the laughing, the hurt and the fun.
Now it's just me and the hard-driven guilt
behind a wall of emptiness I allowed to be built. I'm trapped in my body, just wanting to run back to my youth with its laughter and fun.

By Dave LeFave

We live in a society where there will always be prisons, but we have to ask ourselves is why does it always have to be me; and if we are honest with ourselves the answer will be crystal clear; it doesn't have to be because the choice is ours and ours alone.

The long ride back begin to take a toll on many of us, and then on a summer day in 1995, Governor Parris Glendening gave a press conference in the landscape of the Jessup prison complex, and his announcement would eliminate the chance of any lifer from making parole, and Maryland would become only the third state to require the Governor's signature after the Parole Commission had made their recommendation for release. Therefore, his proclamation of LIFE MEANS LIFE turned a sentence of life into a death sentence for all lifers, creating in de facto a dying breed for those serving life sentences. Clearly, we became political pawns caught up in a system that rewarded people at the polls for their lock them up, throw away the key approach!'

Consequently, their concession is viewed as a premium for punishing prisoners for their prior acts, but totally disregarding any development or rehabilitation; therefore, their philosophy of warehousing men until their geriatric years, and even death, is neither JUDICIOUS OR JUST, and adhering to this approach real justice becomes the first casualty of politics, and to alter the court's ruling from life with the possibility of PAROLE to a sentence of DEATH is beyond the pale of CRUEL AND UNJUST.

There is a saying in print and electronic media, If it bleeds, it leads" We never hear about the thousands of airplanes that land safely every day, but the ones that crash and burn get all the coverage, and so it is with prisoners.

I begin to see too many lose hope, as a result to this policy. Many were becoming battle fatigued; too many unpleasant encounters; too many broken hearts and setbacks; too many children, mothers, and loved ones proceeding them in that awful arena of death, so they call the game and throw in the towel and becomes another statistic and missing face. Perhaps, for them, this is easier than hoping against hope; and without it we die.

Somewhere I recall reading this profound quote: Take from a man his wealth and you hinder him. Take from him his purpose, and you slow him down; but take from him his HOPE, and you stop him. He can go on without wealth, and even without purpose for a while. But he will not go on without HOPE."

So it was with the long ride back, it was certainly impacting our lives to the extent some were beginning to believe that evil and bad always prevail, and our battle cry would become "we almost made it!

During our days at camp we were going outside the fence to work on minimum wages Jobs without supervision. We were paying taxes, obeying all the rules of conduct, and living as law-abiding citizens, and the long ride back was a challenge and text that many were missing the mark and wasting away.

I heard a voice in one ear saying to me, "did you really believe you would leave this place alive? This is the only home you will ever know. You tried to live right and look what it got you.

Don't be a fool; come on back to me, to the booze and the drugs, and I will be your comfort, pleasure, and contentment. Its time you faced reality, Cheese, the good life was never meant for you, so it's time to return to "the good old days"

The sound of the voice was tempting and alluring, but I recognized it to be the voice of deception, and its primary goal was to suggest subtle but treacherous tactics, so I dismissed it as mockery, and I continued to live right, not perfect, but decent and proper.

Some people say that one's movement determines the speed of the clock. My days were full of activity, and I was surprised how fast time seemed to have past. I was approached one afternoon by one of my longtime friends whose name was Paul, and he was scheduled for a parole hearing in the coming days, and it was weighing heavy upon his mind

'I know you've heard I am going before the Commission next week', he said.

"That's a good thing, Paul, and I know you are prepared for this day" Of course, my statement was more of an assumption than it was factual, but he was aware how important preparation was in these hearings. The Commission was a group of men and women from an assortment of professions, appointed by the Governor and approved by the senate, and they determines the release of prisoners, except if you are a lifer; then the Commission can only make a recommendation, and only the Governor has the power to sign his or her release.

I am prepared as I'm going to be, but I still haven't decided what approach to use"

My advice, old friend, is to use the only one that's proven to work"

Which one is that?

Honesty, man, didn't you learn anything from Shawshank Redemption?'

If I use that, I may not never get out of this place"

I know it's a long shot, but not impossible"

We communicated in length on the pros and cons, and we departed in different directions. With the Governor's "no parole' policy for lifers, I was certain he would receive a 3 or 5 year rehearing date, and after his hearing, that's exactly what he received, 5 years. The Parole Commission was very reluctant to issue a recommendation because they knew it would lie on the Governor's desk for more than a year before he rejected it.

Paul's reaction was one of gloom and despondency from the Commission's decision, but that would be pointless in what he would encounter in the coming weeks. I continued to witness some men lose hope, but I also saw in others the amazing thing about their humanity that seemed to rise up within them and convince them better days were still to come, even in the face of great difficulties.

It had been years since the lifers took that dreadful long ride back, but there were still times when I relived it, and replayed it in my conscious, repeatedly. That night is still with me, and I'm not so sure why it is.

I recall celebrating the Bulls defeating the New York Knicks in the six games 6 of the NBA Championship.

Suddenly, the bright lights were brighter than the noonday sun, and the mood quickly shifted from one of celebration to suspicion and trepidation. Everyone became alert as a parade of officers filed into the dorm with a serious and solemn expression and pose.

As they marched into the dorm, they brought with them a sense of fear and alarm. The scene was turning into a nightmare, and terror begin to creep its way into my consciousness. Then, I made the connection; I saw it. Each man who was paid a visit in the dead of night had the misfortune of having a letter attached to his name, LIFE, instead of a number of years.

As we exit the dorm, state police cars surrounded the entire perimeter. Suddenly, I was trembling with fear. 65 lifers stood as if were in a police lineup, and no one could understand why. As I made my way out, I looked into the eyes of sympathetic men who verbalized their sympathy.

Hang in there, Mr. D'

Be strong Brother D'

'Take care Mr. D!'

I pondered the thought, would I ever see any of them again? But they were witness and could give eyewitness account how they came for us in the dead of night. We were 65 lifers, and all that we had accomplished now meant nothing. Good behavior and perfect conduct meant nothing. Most of us had spent 20, 30 and more years working our way through the system, and now we were told it was all for nothing. In essence, the system was rewarding positive behavior with a negative reinforcement, and they justified it all by coming for us that morning.

Somehow I felt like I was traveling back to a time and place that I had made a solemn promise and pledge to never return. But now I had no choice in the matter. As I recalled the long convoy moving toward Hagerstown, I attempted to peep out the window to get some sense of direction, but I was confronted with pitch blackness, which was a perfect symbol of our feelings and mood.

When I first entered the cell and the door locked behind me, I trembled like a leaf on a tree in the autumn breeze. It was a nightmare. I had spent 20 years digging my way out of this horrible grave, and I made sure to pack the dirt tight when I emerged from my tomb. Now I was forced to unearth the soil of my former grave and crawl back into the hole that was deeper now than ever before. How could I do it?

I was hysterical and terror-stricken, and I begin to experience a panic attack. I couldn't breathe; I couldn't get air into my lungs. I felt claustrophobia, and the walls begin to close in on me. I rushed to the window for air, but none entered my lungs. Why was this happening? Tears of anguish and frustration literally fell from my eyes and down my cheeks. Later that morning each of us were interviewed by the prison psychologist to determine if we were suicidal.

But why were we here? Why the long ride back? Was it rational for a system to make 134 men suffer for the guilt of others? Was the criminal behavior of the few police officers guilty of beating Rodney, mean all police were guilty? If one correctional officer is guilty of bringing contraband into the prison, are all to be punished? If one pit bull attacks an individual, are all of them guilty of aggressive and ruthless behavior and punished?

We cannot be responsible for someone else's behavior or actions. Each person must be judged by his or her own behavior, and not by the acts of others; that's rational. There is a danger in this policy or practice. If we are responsible for the behavior of others, then no one is free of guilt.

Months after Paul's decision a small group and me were having a heated discussion about sports, the Ravens, Cowboys, and the Skins.

"The Redskins suck. They're always going to be in the cellar in that division until they get another quarterback!'

"Oh yeah, and your team isn't going anywhere with Romo. I'll take RGIII any day over Romo the bum."

'Man, both of your teams suck. The Ravens are going to the super bowl this year"

You're right; they are going, but they will be sitting in the stands with the rest of the spectators, and they will not be playing in the game"

Unexpectedly, our lively discourse was interrupted by one of our peers. His breathing was labored and strained, and we looked at each other for some indication for his disrespectful interference, but none of us was ready bad news he mumbled.

'We just took Paul to the hospital on a stretcher, and he's in bad shape"

There are days in which we wish would never end; then there are also days in which we would like to expunge events from our consciousness once and for all, and today falls into the latter category.

Several days later, his best friend, Ernest, told us he instructed him to give all of his personal property away. That I didn't understand. Was is instructions premature? Was something going on I did not know or was privy to? Whatever medical condition he had encountered, he would be all right; I was sure of it; that was the opinion and sentiment of us all. But his best friend, Ernest, would die in prison in the year of 2012.

Every day we waited uneasy to hear the report he was recovering, but on day 3, we received the sad and shocking report: He had passed away in the night! What could I do; what could I do in the memory of my longtime friend? In sadness and in tears, I began to write:

IN MEMORY OF MY FRIEND, PAUL

As I sit to write this memorial, I can hear the melodious sounds of a popular jo's song ringing in conscious and the sweet blend of lyrics vibrating in my ears:

How can I say goodbye to what we had?
The good times that made us laugh Outweigh the bad

All I know is where we've been
and what we've been through

If we get to see tomorrow,
I hope it's worth all the wait.
It's so hard to say good bye to yesterday

Some folks die without having really lived, but other folks continue to live in spite of, the fact they have died. Near the end, I believe he was aware that his brief journey of 32 years on the stormy sea of life was drawing to a close. Nevertheless, he was a staunch and robust fighter who had boldly encountered many battles in life, and true to his style and form, he fought this battle to the very end. On July 10, my friend, Paul Manns-El, encountered a mighty, unconquerable foe, and he kept his appointment with death, an appointment that one day, we too must keep.

I first met Paul when he entered the Maryland Pen in the 70s. Our lives soon converged, and we became instant friends, and we grew up and grew old in prison together. We separated during the 80s when he was transferred to Patuxent, and it was doubtful our paths would ever cross again, but upon my arrival in 1993, I was pleasantly surprised to find him here. We both had grown older and became members of the "graying population!"

Life may hold many good qualities and relationships, but the power of death is such that all of the beauty of life is taken away by its grasp.

When I moved into his housing location, our friendship was strengthened and rejuvenated. We talked about having a second chance, a chance often given to those less deserving, only at the expense of those more fitting and justified. We discussed his court case he was fighting to get overturned, and I would say to him:

'Keeping writing and fighting, Paul; keep writing and fighting!'

I'm convinced real, genuine friendships in our environment are few and far between, so we will go to great lengths to protect our sensitive and fragile egos, and we will commit unspeakable acts on each other to mask our weakness, fears, and pain.

The noted author Paul Lawrence Dunbar wrote: "We wear the mask that grin and lie, with torn and bleeding hearts, we smile! YES! We smile only because we know what you see is not what you get."

This in itself is a paradox. To some degree, many would think our common life experiences would serve to unify us; on the contrary, all too often our shared experiences only serve to create more hostility and discord. If you doubt this, all you have to do is see how we treat one another; you will see what we say and do to each other in the name of so-called friendships that is artificial in nature and weak in substance as creek water.

Friendships are precious, and in this environment, they are priceless. I recall very vividly one of my personal struggles, and Paul was there for me in ways I don't even think he understood. I became severely ill and needed abdominal surgery to repair old scar tissue from 3 previous operations. When I returned from Washington County Hospital, and placed in the prison infirmary it was a dark period for me, and there were even times when my own outcome and survival.

I shall never forget that morning when he stopped by the ward to pay me a visit. When he saw my weak and physical condition, I saw the look of concern in his eyes for me. When I slowly tried to get out of bed to greet him, he firmly protested stating I needed to reserve my strength. In every way he demonstrated he was there for me, and when he departed we embraced and he said to me:

I love you, hear. I love you"

Such love and friendship openly displayed made me weep. WOW, I thought to myself, this is all that really mattered. In that moment I realized so many of the commodities we have a tendency to place high priorities on are real cheap, petty, and counterfeit.

Several years later his mother passed, and as soon as I heard the news I rushed to him, just to be there for him and share with him his grief.

'Paul', I said to him, "I just heard about your mom, and I, I," My words choked in my throat, and I began to sob for the loss of his mom, but it was he who had to console me. And now today, it only seemed like yesterday that we stood there reassuring each other everything was going to be all right.

Years later I witness my friend fight perhaps his most difficult battle. He had triple bypass and his recovery was lengthy as well as tedious. He was a long time dialysis patient, a condition that eventually required him to undergo more surgery, from which he never fully recovered.

Each round he fought took its toll and sap his strength until there was nothing left. In his final days, he didn't have energy to walk, and we who loved him had to watch him slowly deteriorate, and there was nothing we could do but pray, and in our own little ways, show him we were there for him.

The reality that weighs on all of life is the certainty of death. No matter who we are, or how long we've lived, we too must face death, and no one will be able to add one day or one minute to this appointment and climatic closing. Death is a door to the existence beyond life, and for those who hope for no other life are dead even in this life.

In the early morning hours of July 10, 1999, my friend, Paul Manns-El, closed his eyes and succumbed to the one battle that he could not win. His passing leaves me with 30 years of memories, memories of a life, of a man, that I had the privilege to call my friend.

And now I hear once again those lyrics ringing peacefully in my ears:

> *And I'll take with me the memories To be my sunshine after the rain It's so hard to say goodbye to YESTERDAY"*

The long ride back was becoming a fading memory, and there was no likelihood of us ever returning to camp again, and if we didn't get redress through the court system, we would become in the words of Sister Helen Prejean, dead men walking.

16

Redemption

A crust of bread and a corner to sleep in,
A minute to smile and an hour to weep in,
A pint of joy to a peck of trouble,
And never to laugh but the moans come double;
And that's life"

(Paul Laurence Dunbar)

TIME CONTINUED TO PAST with the speed of light, and before I realized it, the year was 2004, almost 20 years since our check in and the long ride back. My mother, who has always been my stalwart, continued to make the long trip to visit. On all but two occasions my daughter, Vickie, would accompany her. She was that kind of mother who would put her children first, regardless of their ages. There has never been a time when she had not been there for me. Not long ago I asked God to let me leave this world before her because it would be too hard for me, and I couldn't go on without her. Would God answer my prayer? Maybe so or maybe not, only time would tell.

Each day was full of activities; beginning with prayer, devotion time, 2 hours of power walking, and 200 pushups and setups. I continued to work with our young boys and girls. They came from schools, juvenile facilities, churches, and many of the staff would bring their children. I had been working with them for so many years so inmates would say my name was synonymous with young people.

I will never forget one evening at the close of a session one of the youngsters approached me and put his arm around my shoulder and said, "Man, you really do care about us don't you?"

I looked at him and smiled when I said, "Yes, yes, we all do!"

At first many people thought we were a scared straight program, but there was no comparison between the two. The original award winning Scared Straight of the 70's rapidly became the prototype for most, if not all programs working with youth. It was hailed as a tremendous success earning an academy award for best documentary.

Soon after its debut, inmates rushed forward to form their own youth programs employing their modal. But herein lies a problem for most programs. Somewhere along the way they got trapped in the past. When the problem of our youngsters became myriad and complex, many programs were content to remain unyielding using the original model; and on this account, this distinguished our program from theirs.

Prisoners against Teen Tragedy (PATT), was formed in 1988, and we became a youth diversion and community education program, and at no time do we engage in fear or intimidation. Our goal is never to frighten or terrify, but to encourage them to make better choices. Today's youth are confronted with issues far more complex and complicated than those of the 70s, and the element of fear does not work for them today.

We know these kids can be reached, but the modus operandi must change. A good communicator often changes his method in order to deliver his message, and a good youth program must change its approach if it is to remain relevant with today's youngsters. It must also be perpetually evolving and not become stagnant in the past trying to outdo and outperform the original model. We believe our approach is the right approach for the youth in the twenty-first century.

We know we can reach these youth like no one else can, and when we see that they get the message that is a feeling that's indescribable, and these kids will always be my passion, for our motto in PATT is "because we care."

Whenever I thought I had experience all that life had offer, life had its own way of proving the contrary every single time. I begin to observe more hopelessness, in spite of all the gadgets and devices, accessible. We had game boy, play stations, x-boxes, and other contraption allowing us to escape for a while, but it didn't make us better or improve our present condition.

Prison had in effect become a place where hopelessness was prevalent. Some men were convinced change was beyond their scope, while others didn't see a necessity to do so; consequently, their conduct revealed their despondency and despair; therefore, redemption was beyond their vision because they ascribed to the philosophy such are form was beyond their mental image.

This hopelessness was not exclusive to lifers. I begin to see young boys in large muscular bodies entering without hope. They has lost hope somewhere long before they had to stand before a judge who would passed his judgment. They were beginning a long journey where the odds would be stacked against them, and their frustration was played out in "we wear the mask that grin and lie, with torn and bleeding hearts we smile"

But I can relate to these youngsters because this is the exact way that I came in. I was a smiling man without hope. My mask was to camouflage all that I was not. I had wrongly convinced myself of Paul Laurence Dunbar's:

> "A crust of bread and a corner to sleep in,
> A minute to smile and an hour to weep in,
> A pint of joy to a peck of trouble,
> And never to laugh but the moans come double;
> And that's life"

I recall also reading the words of Martin Luther King, Jr., who articulated these piercing and penetrating words:

"At times we may feel that we do not need God, but on the day when storms of disappointment rage, the winds of disaster blow, and the waves of grief beat against our lives, if we do not have a deep and patient faith our emotional lives will be ripped to shreds."

In the coming months and years, the storms of disappointment would rage; the wave of grief would pound like never before, and my faith would likewise be tested, and I would come to the realization, after all of my dreaming, life was only what I made it.

Thus far, I had experienced many of life's hardships and afflictions: my long bout with cancer, the loss of my brother, my children's mom, my son, and so many other unfavorable circumstances, but soon I would encounter a lost that everything I believed in would be put to the test.

In this life we hope for many things. Those who are ill hope for improved health. The lawbreaker hopes that his punishment will be fair and unbiased. We hope for so many things, but our hope must have an object, and for me, that object was God and the Lord Jesus Christ, but that too would be tested.

When I entered prison in 1974, I served time, but in 1985, my declaration became" I'm man, not made to serve time, be it time was made to serve the man that I'm!' But I still could not rid my conscious of this terrible sense of guilt, the inability to wipe the slate clean and start all over again; although I know, no one is able to redeem time.

There is this scene in the move Shawshank Redemption where the actor Morgan Freeman expressed these words:

I wish I could have a conversation with the young man who put me behind bars for most of my life. I wish I could fix that angry, impulsive kid before prison turned me into an old man!'

As I sat and witnessed his compelling performance, I said to myself, "I, too, wish I could look back at the young man in me, and tell him all that I know now!' In the words of my mother, Junior, my surname, if you keep running with those thugs, you are headed for trouble!' But I refused to pay attention, like so many others of my generation. So I sat locked behind bars longing for another chance, a chance that may never get.

C.S. Lewis once wrote: "Experience is a brutal teacher, but oh how we learn!1 At this stage in my life I thought I had experienced it all; I had encountered it all. But lurking in the shadow of darkness, life would toss me a fast ball, an experience not yet charted, and the victor would be in serious question, and I would come to know and experience the words of Oscar Wilde,

> "Yet each man kills the things he loves,
> The coward does it with a kiss A brave man with a sword."

When I first read those words, I thought I grasp its meaning, but in a brief span of time I would comprehend the meaning, and my heart would shatter into a thousand little pieces.

My movement continued to determine the speed of the clock, and now the year was 2006, and I year I would never forget. Some days I considered to be special in prison, and today was one of those days. The three most important women in my life were: Bernice, my mother; Vickie, my daughter; and Daisy, my sister. And today was a visiting day and I would see two of them, my mother and daughter.

"Cheese, you have a visit," was the announcement over the speakerphone, and I couldn't get there fast enough. As I waited for them to arrive in the visiting room, I thought about my mother and how much I loved her. I heard that God couldn't be everywhere at one time, so that's why He made mothers. Although that is not a factual statement, the implication could not be more accurate. Then, there was my daughter, Vickie, who was only six months old when I left, and now she was a tail and beautiful young women, and I knew it was not easy for her being raised without her father.

As I waited, I begin to reminisce about my adolescent years and mom's wise counsel to prevent me from being in places such as this she now had to visit. She often said, "Junior, a hard head will make a soft rear end' but at the time it was uttered, it didn't quite make sense, but I realize now that 99% of the things she said was truthful.

Finally she entered the large visiting room, but my daughter was not with her, and I was little disappointed for a moment. Instead, our pastor's son, John Wormley Jr., was with her. I noticed she had lost weight, and her eyes scanned the room trying to locate me. Her posture was slightly arched, and she held a walking cane in her right hand for support. She didn't see me yet, and for a moment I thought my eyes were out of focus because I had never seen her as she appeared to me at this moment.

She had been a woman of strength, but always tenderhearted, and she now appeared to be a sheer reflection of the mother of my youthful years. As I fixed my eyes upon her, I suddenly became so full of emotions I struggled to maintain my strong feelings to keep from crying. She had given her children all she had, and she loved us, profoundly! And yet, I had been killing her with the kiss of Oscar Wilde because I was a coward, and lived a life that now stained the character of her love.

She finally saw me, and her countenance was radiant with an enormous smile upon her fragile face. Step by step she moved toward me with a noticeable shiver in her legs. Slowly, she continued moving, step by step, and I could no longer hold back the warm tears as I thought about all of the pain I caused her in life, unknowingly and unintentionally. I wanted to tell her how sorry I was u but the prison rules restrained me to my seat, and the tears gradually moved down the side of my cheek. How could I have been so blind and foolish? How could I?

My sister told me when she received my letters she would go into her bedroom and close the door, and she would hear her weeping behind closed doors. As I now ponder her words, I wonder how many sons at this very moment are killing their mothers or loved one with a kiss, the kiss of Oscar Wilde?

She reaches me, finally, and I kissed her on the cheek, told her I loved her, and held her for a long time in her motherly, warm embrace.

I told Vickie what time I was leaving, and I couldn't keep John waiting all day, was her first words.

"It's all right, mom; it's all right," I said.

We talked; we laughed, and after all of these years, being in her presence was still majestic. A mother knows her children, so she knew I was a little let down that Vickie wasn't with her, but she told me how well she was doing.

She was employed, had her own apartment, and she never caused me the pain that I caused my mother. I knew how difficult it was for a child to be raised in the absence of their fathers, but I was floored when I read the stats:

> 85% exhibit behavioral disorders.
> 73% drop out of high school
> 75% are in adolescents and treatment centers.
> 75% are juveniles in state institutions.
> 85% are youth in adult prison.
> 82% of all teenage girls who get pregnant are from fatherless home.

YES, I was proud of my daughter for the young woman she had become, in spite of my absence. Finally our visit was terminated, and I kissed her again, and told her I loved her. Those were always our last words whenever we communicated in person, by phone or by letters.

I watched her walk away; she turned and waved goodbye, and that was the last time I would see her alive. The sum of all fears is the fear of death, the final loss of control. While we might be able to avoid some of the lesser losses in life; in the end, we must all come to grips with the fact that no one cheats death. And so it was on November 2006, my mother suffered a stroke and remained in a comma until December 30, one day before her 83rd birthday when she slipped away in the night, and went home to glory to be with the Lord. I'm told the loss of a child or mother is the most painful loss of all, and now I have lost both, a son and a mother, and I cried out in a loud voice, when will this all end?

They say time heals all wounds, but that's a maxim I can no longer trust or accept as true. Approaching the fifth anniversary of her passing, and my pain has not eased or lessen, and is now my lifelong companion. I tell myself it doesn't supposed to be this hard and unrelenting, but my mind still cannot grasp her absence in my life, and my mind and body just will not let me forget.

There are actually a few moments when I try to convince myself I have actually come to terms with it, but there are situations, visual sights and audible sounds of her that flood my memory, and I lose the battle to hold back the tears, and I wonder does yesterday have to last forever.

OH, how I miss her presence in my life. Years later I would still find the task of reading too hard to concentrate. There was so much I didn't have the chance to tell her, but I believe she knew even if those words remained unspoken. Even though her appearance has somewhat diminished, her picture reveals a life of struggle and self sacrifice. There are days when I appear strong, but internally there's a turbulence raging within, and I'm confronted with the reality, she is gone and nothing for me could ever be the same.

She never gave up on me, even when she has legitimate reasons to do so. Only a mother knows their children better than anyone else but God, and they can see through our disguises.

I thank God for allowing her to live long enough to see me come to the cross and receive salvation, and see Him transform my life forever; and that had to be one of the happiest days of her life, and now I live to honor her legacy.

Facing the truth about ourselves is not a place we arrive at easy. For most of my life it was always someone else responsible for my troubles and problems, so as long as I held that view, redemption was unattainable and inconceivable. On October 7, 1985, I hit rock bottom, and that is when Jesus walked into my world with a sparkle in HIS eye and gave me an offer I could not refuse or resist:

"Sit still for a while," He says, "I can do wonders with this mess of yours."

He walked into my life and took away the guilt, the shame, the disappointments, and the pain. He changed my life from the inside out. What others saw as a mess He saw something entirely different, and with Him no one is beyond the power of REDEMPTION.

In the words of Ralph Waldo Emerson: "Everyone is entitled to be judged by his best moments."

It has been 40 years since I entered prison, and by all accounts I should have died decades ago with Tank, Alonzo, Glen, Jerome, Amend, Donald, William, George, Lewis, Ralph, Arthur, Oscar, Greg, and so many, many others.

To my knowledge most of these men died without Christ. In the book, STRENGTH OF LOVE, Martin Luther King, Jr. wrote, "In a generation of so many colossal disappointments, men have lost faith in God, faith in men, and faith in the future. But earth has no problems that heaven cannot heal."

There is a great need for all people to know that in our world of so much loneliness and despair, there is a God that forgives, that cares, and wants to heal all that is broken, and we need not walk through life alone.

For 40 years the doors of my release remained bolted shut. The Circuit and Appellate Courts were also closed. I filed countless petitions, and were denied stating "without merits." Also, with the current no parole policy initiated by Gov. Glendening now acknowledged his action was more motivated by politics than any hard evidence it would make the public safer, his predecessors continues to enforce and maintain his edict, and lifers continues to die in large numbers.

All of the doors were closed and all avenues exhausted, but I still maintained my faith and hope in God. On October n, 2012, Brain M. Saccenti, Chief Attorney of the Appellate Division, filed a motion to the Circuit Court to reconsider a motion I had filed pro se that had been denied. Shortly thereafter, the Court issued an order granting our motion and a hearing was scheduled for April 23, 2013.

In March 2U3, my friend Hardy "Fat Man" Herring, was still in the prison hospital. He had completed chemotherapy treatment for stomach cancer.

Ira, perhaps his best friend, received word from his sister that the cancer had spread to his liver and bones, and his condition was now terminal.

Immediately we wanted to see him, and our wish was granted when Sgt. V escorted Ira, Phillip, and I to see him for five minutes. As we walked there, I thought about our friendship of 38 years and how we met. He arrived in prison several years after me and our lifestyles of boozing and drugs sealed our relationship, and we became good friends.

Sometime during the year of '83, he suddenly stopped using and drinking without a hint or notification, and I observed him become a different person. I asked him one day, "Fat Man, what's up with you?" His answer was astonishing when he begin to tell me about Jesus and him being saved.

Jesus! What was this nonsense? To me, Jesus was nothing more than a theological concept and a religion for the weak. But as time passed, I could not deny the miraculous change I saw in him, and it was something that I wanted. Whatever it was, I knew if it worked for him, it would also work for me. But it would take several more years of boozing and drugging for me to have my own personal encounter with the Lord Jesus Christ. He was no longer a concept, but the Son of a living God with the power of redemption and power to transform any life.

The sergeant and the three of us entered the infirmary. He was lying in the last bed with his eyes closed, and his appearance was a reflection of his condition. His surname was "Fat Man", but his ailment reduced him to flesh and bones, a shell of his former self.

Ira moved to the right of his bed while Phillip and I went to the left. His eyes were closed when Phil softly whispered his name, "Hardy, Hardy."

He slowly opened his eyes, glancing to both sides of the bed, as our recognition brought a smile upon his parched lips, and he spoke each of our names. I knelt beside the bed to hold his hand, and I believe just by being there, even in our moments of silence, were the loudest words that were spoken.

He said all he needed were our prayers; then he spoke words that reassured us he was in the right place and he had found his way back home.

"If the death angels come for me, I'll be singing in glory."

His eyes were full of tears, as he tried to dry them. I saw in his feeble eyes a look I shall never forget, and our hearts were full of compassion for our beloved brother. Still on my knees, he pulled me to him as I kissed his cheek and caressed his head. Then I stood upright, took several steps backwards, buried my face into my wool cap and silently wept. My friend, my dear friend, how did our lives bring us to this time and place?

As we left the ward, I knew this could very well be me lying there in his condition. It was only by the grace of God I had been spared a little more time to perhaps be used for His glory and the benefit of His people. But one day, I too, must fold up this tent and time for me will be no more.

We are more than Solomon Grundy: Born on Monday, christened on Tuesday, married on Wednesday, took ill on Thursday, worse on Friday, died on Saturday, buried on Sunday, and that was the end of Solomon Grundy.

Living 40 years in the bowls of the beast with crisis after crisis at every turn. Ordinarily men don't have a life span that allow them to reach their senior years because their demise is precipitated by a destructive lifestyle. My brother, my son, and my mother are all gone, but I stand firmly on the declaration that faith is knowing God is present even when all we hear is silence.

I saw her again. She was the same beautiful woman I had seen in the restaurant, but this time she became visible in last night's dream. She was fashionable dressed and the same picture of elegance and class, but when I tried to approach her, she vanished like a puff of smoke. What is it about her that makes her show up in dreams and imagination? She will be back, I tell myself, and she will no longer exist in dreams and imaginary.

It was June 2015, and for the first time in my experiences I would walk into the Circuit Court of Prince George's County with a hopeful and optimistic outlook. Today would determine if I would die in prison like so many of my cherished friends, or would I be granted mercy and a second chance to live the life as a free man after so many years.

When my court date was publicized, many came by to wish success, but not everyone is man enough to celebrate another man's victory and success, but for those who did I knew it was authentic and for real.

STATE OF MARYLAND V. CHEESE

My attorney was Brian M. Saccenti, Chief Attorney of the Appellate Division, and the door was opened in the case of UNGER V. STATE where the jury was given "advisory only" instructions violating the presumption of innocence and reasonable doubt standard.

My attorney argument was the trial judge muddled the judge/jury dichotomy and erred in instructing the jury as to its role as trier of the law and the facts, and it would be intolerably unjust to require me to spend the rest of my life in prison based on a trial where the jury was authorized to depart from fundamental due process requirements.

Over the years I had my share of attorneys, but none as skilled and well prepared as Mr. Saccenti, and over the weeks to come the nature of our relationships was altered from attorney and client, to one of mutual friends.

He communicated the judge would accept the State's offer to life suspended all but 40 years; thereby, making it possible to exist the court a free man. Although he was confident of today's proceedings, he was also familiar with Murphy's Law, so there could be no premature celebration until the judge s decision was announced in court and recorded into the records.

As I paced the holding cell in the Prince George's County Circuit Court, I anxiously awaited for the deputy to escort me into the courtroom to face the judge who would determine my fate.

And as waited, I vividly remembered a documentary on PBS I had seen years ago. It was about animals taken from their natural environment and placed in captivity, an unnatural habitat.

As they observed the animals, they discovered they begin to exhibit unusual behaviors. The large elephant begin to shift his weight from one leg to another in a rocking motion, what they labeled as the "dance of death". Then there was a giraffe who spent long hours doing nothing but licking the bark of trees. Suddenly I had an epiphany. If animals were affected by an unnatural habitat, how much more would it affect humans, and there is no other environment more unnatural than that of prisons; and its affects are even more disastrous and catastrophe.

During my first hearing my attorney argued my case, and my sister, Daisy; my best friend, Mark; my cousin, Dot; and John were all present in the courtroom. On my second hearing, I was not present because an error was made by the clerk, but my presence was not necessary, and the judge agreed with my attorney and the prosecutor to suspend my sentence. But today was the day I had been praying for, year after year.

It was after 9am when I was ushered into the courtroom, and I was relieved to see my supporters on the front row. Mr. Saccenti had presented the prosecutor with a thick profile of my accomplishments, programs and organizations, prison adjustment, academic, and letters of recommendations from the highest prison officials, and the judge's decision was based this information.

As I stood before the Honorable Judge Whalen, I plead guilty and my new sentence was life suspended but 40 years and one day probation. "Do you accept the conditions", was the judge's answer.

"Yes, your honor," was my quick replay.

Although my answer was affirmative, I asked my attorney, "What does one day probation mean."

"All it means," he said, "Stay out of trouble overnight, and you don't have to report to anyone and there are no restrictions."

"WOW", I deeply exhaled, "I'm free! I'm free!" my mind was racing 1000 miles an hour and I am trying to process what this all means when the female prosecutor moved toward me with her right hand extended.

"May I shake your hand,"

"You certainly may," I smiled.

Mr. Saccenti later told me she was not the kind of prosecutor whose ambition was to rack up convictions, but her purpose was to see that justice was administered, and to me that spoke volumes. When I was about to greet my family and head for the exit door, the deputy came forward with his handcuffs out and gave the command to put my hands behind my back.

"What are you doing," was my attorney's question, "didn't you hear the judge's decision?"

"Yes, but they are never released from the court. He has to return to prison for them to complete the paper work, which will take several days."

By his none verbal communication and expression, I knew his answer was unacceptable. "I'll be down to see you in a few", he said as I was led back to the holding cell.

In route there he said, "Where did you find that lawyer? He had to cost you a pretty penny, didn't he?"

"Believe it or not, he didn't cost me a cent. He is the chief attorney in the public defender's office."

"Get out of here", was his response as I entered the cell.

Just before I left the cell I was introduced to a young brother from western Maryland who was also there seeking a new trial. "How did it go", he wanted to know.

"The judge gave me time served". Before I realized it, he gave me a big embrace saying, "I am glad for you, so glad for you", was his words.

He also had a life sentence, and had less than 10 years in, and we talked about the positive things he was doing, and I encouraged him to continue doing good, regardless of today's outcome.

In my mind I had prepared to leave the court a free man. I knew my return would only be for a few days, but I just wasn't prepared to go back, not even for an hour. But while I awaited to be transported back to prison, I tried to keep my mind occupied, and I wanted to leave my temporary mate with a positive message, so our discussion shifted to the imperative of having a plan in life; and without a plan, we plan to fail.

Jack Olson writes about a plan in terms of a gimmick, and records: "For some it is narcotics.

For others it is crime. For more than a few, the only gimmick that seem feasible is sports. The black athlete who fails to become Wilt, Elgin, or an Oscar finds himself competing for employment in an economic market that has little use for the breakaway dribble and fade away jump shot." In this world, the slam dunk is counterfeit.

Approximately one and a half hour later, the slot to the door was opened, and the transportation officer said in a rather excited tone, "It's been approved!"

For some reason, I didn't hear him correctly, so I asked to repeat what he said, "What did you say? Did you say it was disapproved?"

"No," was his reply. "I said it has been approved, and you are out of here in about 15 minutes."

I was so full of excitement I thought I would literally lose conscious. In less than 15 minutes, the same officer returned and unlocked the cell. "Come on Cheese; it's time for you to leave, but first give me your DOC (Division of Correction) shirt and then your prison identification." When I complied, he said I could leave, pointing at the rear door.

Several times I glanced back, as looking for directions, and he kept pointing and as he followed me from a distance. I existed the building and came to the parking lot. I wasn't sure what direction to go, and I heard him say, "Take a left, and another left, and you will be at the front of the court." Every few paces I would look back, as he continued to point.

I am jubilant, overjoyed, ecstatic, excited, and a thousand similar emotions, right? Absolutely not; not even close. I'm frighten to death. As I made my way to the front of the building I am trembling with fear and in a panic mode. I look around at all of these strange people, all of these strange faces. I have no money and don't know how to find home, and I suddenly had my Shawshank Redemption moment, and I thought for a brief moment, at least back in prison, I wouldn't have to face all of these strange, new challenges.

"Would you please call a number for me," I asked, "I was just released from court and I don't have any money, and don't know how to get home."

I gave him my best friend, Mark's, number I had committed to memory, he dialed the number and gave me the phone. What was I supposed to do? What end do I talk or speak in? I had never seen a cell phone before. When he instructed me how to use it, my voice was full of fear as I told Mark I had just been released, but it went to his voice mail, and my sense of fear intensified a hundredfold. What was I to do? I couldn't call home because I knew my sister had not returned from court, and Mark couldn't be here because of his job obligation.

Suddenly, in my periphery vision, I saw my attorney running toward me in the sweltering heat of July with a huge smile upon his face and his collar was soaked in perspiration. He gave me a big bear hug also, and turned toward the building and said, "Now, let's go meet your family."

To my surprise, my sister, John, and Dot was slowly running to meet me, and my attorney took pictures from a gadget that I later learned was a tablet. Before he departed he gave me instructions: "Go home. Don't go anywhere for a few days, enjoy your family, and call me Monday because I want to know how you are doing".

I stood there thinking, *What an introduction, Cheese! What an introduction—now welcome home! Welcome to the "free world."* But I had a gut feeling that I hadn't seen anything yet. FREEDOM can be a scary proposition, especially after 4 decades in prison.

I was to reside with my sister and her two sons until I was able to support myself and find an affordable pad of my own, but that in itself was more difficult than I anticipated. Only a few people knew that I was home, not even my daughter. She knew that I had a court appearance, but no idea I was coming home.

I was released on Thursday, and on Saturday Mark came over to take me shopping for clothes. "How does it feel to be home, Cheese?"

"I don't think it had hit me yet."

"That's normal, considering how long you have been away, it will come to you."

Our first stop was Costco, and we pulled into the biggest customer parking lot I had ever seen, when we entered the size of it was enormous and the people innumerable. As long as he remained in my line of vision, I was good, but when he disappeared out of sight I was overwhelm with fear, and remained in that state until saw him.

He purchased three set of clothing from there, and our next stop was Walmart, another extremely large store, and from there we had lunch, and I stayed with him until late afternoon when he dropped me off.

"Junior," my sister called from upstairs, "Vickie is on the phone."

It had been a long time since I saw her, and too long since we had communicated, but when my mother was alive we had almost daily communication, and now there was so much say and do.

"Hi, sweetheart," was my first words to her, "how have you been?"

"I am angry with you, Dad. Why didn't you let me know you were home? And when am I going to see you?"

"I have only been home for two days, and Daisy and no one had your recent number. We finally got it from your grandmother. I have only been out of the house once."

"The Fourth of July is a few day off, and I want to come over and spend all day with you."

"That will be good, Vick, and I am dying to see you without any restriction, as it was in prison."

We talked for more than an hour, and she is the one I would spend most of my time with. She had an apartment in Southeast, and it took two buses and almost 90 minutes, depending on the day and hour.

Before I realized it the holiday had arrived and I was eager to spend the day with Vickie. Daisy spent the morning in the kitchen preparing a delicious and mouth-watering meal. She arrived late in the morning, and I was looking out the window when she climbed the steps. I opened the door wide, and she walked into her father s arms, all smiles.

We ate the tasty and luscious meal Daisy had prepared, and we retired to the basement trying to make up for time lost that could never be redeemed. Daisy prepared a plate for her to take home, and it was time to say goodbye, but I would come to spend more time at her house than I did my own.

Every Sunday I went to church with Daisy. It had been my family's small church for many, but I would also go with Mark to his church, First Baptist Church of Glenarden which I would later join.

Pastor Nancy Engen called and we would talk, after she would pray with and for me. Ladell came down from Baltimore and took me to lunch at Red Lobsters. My friend, Larry Gaither, and I spent time together, and I attended his wedding. Ahmed, my friend, who lived in Leisure World, took my daughter and I to lunch, and he gave me a computer and printer and many items of clothes. My aunt Flo took me to P. G. Plaza Mall and purchased three suits for me. I couldn't get over how nice everyone was, and Dave Manley came down and took me to lunch with his two sons. YES, it was beginning to feel like home.

In August, Mr. Saccenti asked if I would give an interview by the Washington Post, which I consented, gladly. Everyone didn't think it would be a good idea, but I disagreed and gave the interview, and it was one of the best decision I made since my homecoming.

When I agreed, I thought it would only take a day, perhaps two at the most, but it took one year to complete. They followed me practically everywhere I went: church, computer class, job training, driving test, at my daughter's apartment, with my best friend, Mark, at the house with friends, Christmas play at FBCG(First Baptist Church Glenarden), and it was countless interviews.

The reporter was Lynh Bui, Marvin Joseph, photographer, and Whitney Leaning, video journalist.

It was actually two interviews; one for the newspaper, and the other for their website. The article was finally printed in The Washington Post on Sunday, July 20, 2014, front page on the metro section.

Each Night, I Die

I was a veteran of many hard fought battles, but my worst battles were still yet to come. In prison the fight was mostly single, the institution; but in the real world the war arena and combat is more intense, and it comes from every angle, stalking my every move. I thought I had slain the beast, but that creature that lies in each of us is not so easily defeated.

I was confronted with numerous real life problems, ordinary problems, yet foreign to me, but I would have to deal with them, for I had an invisible foe seeking to turn my real life into a tragedy, and rendering me useless and nonfunctional.

My sister and I have always been closer than Siamese twins, but upon my release we would have to re-acquaint ourselves, but that in itself would be a challenge and also take time. Then, there was my daughter, Vickie, who had the potential to be my greatest impediment, by no fault of her own; and that too, would take time and hard work.

Remember, when I left she was only 6 months old, but when I returned home she was 40 years of age, and In my head I had created this perfect little girl without flaws or shortcomings. Even when she came to visit me with my mother, she was still a child of perfection, daddy's little girl, but how could I know at the time it was all a fallacy?

In the coming months it would take a personal crisis for me to see her as she really was: sometimes weak, other times strong; sometimes vague, other times clear and precise; sometimes vain, other times meek and humble; conceited, yet caring and concerned. Her flawless coat of perfection begin to fade like a distant memory of the past, and today I'm forced to reconcile facts with fiction, and for the first time in 40 years, I see her as she really is.

I see her pain unspoken, past experiences she would like to erase or blot from her memory forever, secrets buried deep into her conscious she could never reveal; but most of all I see her yearning for a Dad, a dad she never had.

I'm home at last, but I had ideal what fatherhood was all about. It was totally foreign and new territory to me, and I had no reference to use as a guide or model. Being a father long distant is

235

no comparison to being one up close and personal, and my most difficult daily task remained one of guilt and being missing in action (MIA), when she and her brother needed a father the most, and I can never turn back the clock and start life over again.

My daughter would have to introduce her dad to the world of technology. She would go with me to purchase my first cell phone, and patiently instructed me how to use it, including how to text and send emails. She would even have to teach me to ride the subway and read the signs getting from one part of the city to the other. More than once riding up or down the escalators she had to tell me, "Dad, you have to stand to the right and leave the left side open for those who are passing."

Mark and I went to the Verizon Center to see the Mystics V. Indiana Fever. His wife, Sue, later joined us at Oriental East for a fantastic meal in City Place, located in Silver Spring, Maryland. John Jr. and I attended an 8 week Men's Enrichment Session at Mt. Pleasant Baptist, and then we joined Mark for communion night at First Baptist Church Glenarden where the guest Preacher was the Re. Dr. Richard A. Farmer.

I went to the historic Rally for Jobs & Justice on the Mall, for the 50th Anniversary of Dr. Martin Luther King's march on Washington. Ladell came down again from Baltimore, and we went to Pier 7 for lunch, but I continued to spend the bulk of my time with Vickie in Southeast.

One day when I returned from her apartment to my basement, I begin to feel discontented and overburden. Suddenly I was overwhelm with the issues of life and living, and nothing seemed to made sense anymore. And for the first time in my life I became completely unraveled, and suddenly I begin to shed tears and softly mourn, but with every breath, my voice and cry became louder and louder, and I collapsed on the floor on my knees screaming, "I want my mother! I want my mother!"

My sister descend the stairs trying to console me, but I kept repeating the same four words, "I want my mother," and it felt like I was losing my mind, but it was the beginning of a secret I kept for

Each Night, I Die

six months, and later diagnosed as manic depression. It is a disease that would require medication and treatment from Dr. Bland and mental health staff at Howard University Hospital.

It would attack me at any time, and I didn't seem to have a weapon to defend myself, leaving me defenseless. I'm in trouble again, I would say; and no one must know about it. Externally I look good, but internally I am coming apart and don't know what to do.

I visit these places, deep, dark places and I am afraid to be alone. My head is spinning and I feel this pressure that is crushing me from the inside out, but no one must know, I tell myself.

It's my big secret; and it's killing me. I have come as close to death as anyone can possibly come. Living is tough, but dying is even harder. I, Cheese, is suffering from depression, and the stigma associated with the disease made me keep in a secret longer than I should have, and now I am getting better, and I can live with it the same as a diabetic can live with diabetes.

It has been 2 years since my release, but I can't get over how much the city has changed. It is no longer "chocolate city ", but one of racial and culture ethnicity. No one would believe how they have transformed 14th Street, and now they are doing the same to H Street N.E. The architectural structure of some of the buildings is impressive.

I received the sad news that my dear friend, Hardy "Fat Man" Hearing, passed away in the prison infirmary from cancer after 38 years behind the fence. There is still a need for prison reform, and trying to solve the problem by building more hospitals is like trying to solve the AIDS problem by building more hospitals.

In The Washington Post, Sunday, August 16, 2015 reported these stats on the need for prison reform:

2.3 Million

The nation's prison and jail population today, more than quadrupled from 3000.000 in 1980. The United States has less than 5 percent of the world's population but nearly a quarter of the world's prison population.

1 in 100

Adults behind bars in America. As many as 2 million of all American adults now have a criminal history record.

60 Percent

Of prisoners today are people of color. One in 3 black men face the likelihood of imprisonment, and black men are six times as likely to be incarcerated as white men, while Hispanic men are 2.5 times as likely.

$80 billion

Amount the federal government spends each year on prisons, nearly a third of the Justice Department's budget. Between 2000 to 2013, the cost per federal inmate increased by almost $8,000, resulting in a $2.3 billion increase in the Bureau of Prisons' budget.

400 percent

Growth in states' combined corrections spending from 1980 to 2009.
Anthony Kennedy, then the Supreme Court Justice, was addressing the American Bar Association in 2003, urged them to study the inadequacies and injustices in our prison and correctional system… our resources are misspent, our punishment too severe, and sentences too long.
When I came home, I said I wanted a cell phone, an automobile, a job, and a wife. Today, only two remain on that list, a wife and apartment. Also, I promised I would visit the gravesite of those I lost, but never really had the chance to say goodbye; and recently
I kept that promise, and my daughter wanted to accompany me.

Each Night, I Die

On our way to Glenwood Cemetery located in Northeast we stopped to pick up flowers. Her mother was my first love, and we were together for 5 years when I was first arrested. When we arrived at the burial ground, I placed a small bouquet on the mount of earth, and I imagined what our lives would have been if she was still alive. I thought about our laughter and the good times, and the love she gave me that would make any man feel like a king. We had our bad times, but they were offset by the pleasant and lively days.

Shortly after we met I recall reading a poem in a lonely prison cell, and thoughts of her would flood my mind:

> *"There will be new dreams,*
> *Replacing those that fell apart,*
> *For life is never what it seems.*
> *There will be new hope,*
> *To mend a child's broken heart;*
> *For love is made of broken dreams."*

And now all I have of her are memories, memories of a time and place that we once lived so very long ago. You were that prize, Jean, that I lived all my life to win, and now you are gone.

Not far from her burial place was my/our son whose peers tagged as "Big Dave." Vickie and I had to pause for a brief spell because we knew it would not get any easier. They had been as close as my sister and. He was 4 years older than she, and he was that big-brotherly guard who watched over and protected her.

When we reached the short distance separating them in death, she begin to talk to him as if he was still among the living. I knelt and placed flowers on his grave, and we both wept; she for a brother, and I for a son, also gone too soon and placed in the cold bosom of soil that now served as his final place of residence.

One more site to go, and perhaps the hardest of all for me. First, I asked myself was I ready for this day, and the answer was I had no other choice. Arriving at our destination, Fort Lincoln, it was late afternoon. The attendant gave us a map with directions on how to locate site, but it still took Vickie and I a minute to find it. There it was beneath an enormous bronze stature with arms extending toward heaven, and I thought, what a perfect place to rest.

There was so much I wanted to tell her, how sorry I was for not being a better and obedient son, and suddenly tears of regret and sadness fell freely from my eyes, "I'm home now, Mom; I am home, but oh how I miss you, but I believe it's going to be all right, because this time I found our long lost promise land."

Every time we communicated on the phone she would always say to me, "I am trying to hold on till you come home." And with every letter she would write, "Keep your faith, Son, and trust in God."

When we left, I felt relieved because I had come to say goodbye. My daughter and I realized we would encounter barriers on the road to our destiny, but they would make us better, not bitter, for there would be a purpose for my pain, and a testimony in my test.

It has been 2 years since I have been home, and I'm still adjusting to my new found freedom. Everything is electronically, and all you have to do is swipe a card, and everything is at his or her disposal.

I am blessed to have had friends who were there for me, to walk with me, take my hand and demonstrate how things are done. But there comes a point in time when they will have to release your hand, and that in itself can be a frightening endeavor. They have jobs, families, and other responsibilities, but I know they will always be there for me, and today I am learning to walk alone with their support.

Mark has been that kind of friend that everyone should have at least one in the course of a life time. I can't count the times when I heard, "Cheese, are you in a group? Cheese, you have to get in a group." "Cheese, what are you waiting for?" But that's what true friends do. It might not be what you want to hear, but it's what you need. Isn't that's what friends are for?

I finally accepted his advice, and I am in two men's focus group at church, and I truly understand the value of participating in a men's group, and it is exactly what I need. Dr. Parker says, "A man can't know himself, grow himself, by himself." He also says, "If you are the star in your dream, it is a nightmare." Life is too tough for any man to do it alone.

As I viewed the obstacles and challenges that coexist with freedom, I composed it in a composition "I'm Still Here".

I'M STILL HERE— I believe one of life's many lessons has been yesterday can last forever. I've heard time heals all wounds, but I cannot ascribe to that expression because reality proves otherwise. TIME is an awesome term, but it can also be a frightening place to live, especially if that place is prison, where I lived for 40 years.

They said no one could do it; no one could possibly live that long in the belly of the beast, not even me. If I did come out, the odds would be 100 to 1 against me that the rapid currents of the technology world would leave me in a state of "limbo" and yearning to return to the days of yesterday.

BUT I'M STILL HERE— I have lived all of my life for this moment, and no one can stop me, but me; and I refuse to go away. Doing time, I saw first hand the vicious acts committed by man, against man. I walked through valleys so deep and dark it literally drove some men mad. To cope with this madness, I tried to dull my pain with the "sweet wine" of the ages, and later became addicted to the poison plant of the poppy seed.

BUT I'M STILL HERE— I have been pushed to the brink of a mental breakdown, and I have seen my loved ones precede me into the awful arena of death.

BUT I'M STILL HERE— For every lost suffered, there has also been a lesson learned. Today, I am no longer identified by a six digest number. Two years ago, on June 27, 2013, the judge reduced my life sentence to 40 years time served, with no restrictions. Is there a parallel in my engagement since I am on this side of the fence? Absolutely! Because I'm free, it does not close the door to conflict. Freedom is never FREE because it comes with a price tag.

BUT I'M STILL HERE— Today; the battles are different, more intense; and they come from all directions and angles, and where we think we are strongest the battle can reveal as our weakness. Benjamin E. Mays wrote, It isn't a calamity to die with dreams unfulfilled, but it is calamity not to dream." We struggle with fear, doubt, faith, death, failure, and many others. Sometimes we triumph, but other times they get the upper hand. But that's all right, for we continue to fight no matter what. The battle may be over, but the war continues.

BUT I'M STILL HERE— My issues may not be same as yours, but as long as we are above the ground, we will encounter conflict. In many way I am no different from most of America, because we are connected by our struggles, the ones we attempt to camouflage, conceal, disguise, and deny exist. The crime for which I committed is what I did, not who I am, but if you see me through the prism of your own prejudice, bigotry, intolerance, and bias you will not see the person that I am, and you will leave this world knowing less about me as those did yesterday when they crossed the street when they saw me coming. There are good days, and those that are not that good.

BUT I'M STILL HERE— "If you know the enemy and yourself, you will not fear too battles. If you know yourself and not the enemy, for every victory you will suffer a defeat. If you know neither yourself nor the enemy, you are a fool and you will meet defeat in every battle." (Sun-tzu, sixth century Chinese General).

That has been my second greatest life's lesson. I have always been my own worst enemy, but no one can stop me now and losing is not an option, and that's why I can say,

I'M STILL HERE!

Because I have been a recipient of God's grace, no one can deny the truth because I'm living proof that Jesus Christ can repair the broken and shattered pieces in our lives. He can renew, restore, and resurrect the dead and useless things we don't know what to do with. Regardless of who you are, or what you may have done, no one is beyond His power of redemption.

A guilty conscious is a body breaking load, and there at the cross Jesus Christ set me free from the guilt and the shame that made me an enemy of myself and of others. Saint Augustine said it well when he wrote:

Each Night, I Die

"O Lord you have made us for Yourself,
And our hearts are restless till they rest in You."
Your love is greater than our guilt and wrongdoing. Your love is greater than our weakness. Save us from all the things that enslave us;
more importantly, save us from ourselves.

I recall some years ago after my daughter read the open letter to my son, she asked a very candid question. "Daddy, where is my letter?" It was a valid question, but at the time I don't believe she understood the circumstances surrounding that letter. Now, after many years have passed, I sat down to answer her question; although under different circumstances, but just as poignant and just as heart rendering.

A PERSONAL LETTER TO MY DAUGHTER

Growing up in the South as a small boy, my life's ambition was not like those of most boys my age. My desire wasn't to become a doctor, attorney, athlete, or any of those noble vocations. No, my primary goal was simply to become a father.

Perhaps, this goal was rooted in my childhood when my father and mother separated, and she would have to rear three small children all alone; it was then I made a solemn promise to myself, if I ever became a father, my children would never be without their dad. In 1969, your brother was born, and I believe I was the world's most jubilant father. But this was a time when I was caught up in the inner city drug trade, and I foolishly allowed his young eyes to see things he should have never seen.

Three years later, you were born, and by this time my reckless life was completely out of control. I was not only selling drugs, but I had also become addicted, and my addiction was like making love to a gorilla, and you're never through till the gorilla says you are through.

Your birth was a blessing, my daughter, and a perfect time for me to look at the cards I was holding and to see it was a losing hand. This was the perfect time for me to toss my cards on the table and walk away, never to return to the game again; but I didn't. I continued to return, time after time, trying to turn a lousy pair of deuces into a royal straight flesh. You see, the gorilla, wasn't through yet.

In 1972, six months after your birth, I was arrested for murder and sentenced to life in prison, and clearly it was the judge's intent for me to never leave alive. Upon my arrival, I was reminded of the words of Oscar Wilde who once wrote; "We always hurt the ones we love. The brave man kills with a sword, but a coward kills with a kiss." And I became acquainted with so many other men who were killing the ones they loved with a kiss, exactly like me, and here I was destine to die behind four gigantic, concrete walls.

I reiterate, no experience can prepare one for a life in prison. It is a hell that knows no mercy. It is a million dreams that will never be fulfilled. It is too many tears without laughter; too much darkness without light, and this was to be my world for 40 long, painful years.

Grasping I was to never go home, my days were consumed with drugs, booze, and hustling. The gorilla still wasn't through, so this would be my existence for thirteen more years. The noted author Paul Laurence Dunbar, wrote:

> "We wear the mask that grin and lie, with torn and bleeding hearts, we smile." We smile because we know what you see is not what you get, so we wear the mask to camouflage our weakness, our pain, and our insecurities.

The hardest part of your father's prison life was being separated from you and your brother, yet nothing could slow me down, not even cancer. In 1979, I was diagnosis with liver cancer, but after four months of chemotherapy, the doctors could not find any trace of the disease, so I was released from the prison infirmary back into the prison population.

This should have been enough for your father to do some self-examination, but it wasn't. I couldn't wait to get back into the "rat race." What would it take for me to learn? It would take six more agonizing years of drugging and boozing for me to hit rock bottom, and I remember crying out to the Lord that October morning I could not live another day in my present condition, and if this was all that life had to offer, then it just wasn't worth living; and there in all of my pain, loneliness, and near madness, I found a Savior that loved me more than my earthly mind could comprehend, and that was the first day and first page in your father's life and discourse.

Every day I thought about you and your brother, as our communication was restricted to letters, phone calls, and visits. I didn't know that your brother had become a major player in the drug trade until he made the front page of the Washington Post. As you know, he was charged with two murders and distribution, but found not guilty of the murders, but sentenced to 30 years for distribution.

As I read about his reckless and violent life, I saw a picture of myself, and I was overcome with guilt. I should have seen it coming because the die was cast while he was still in the cradle.

I wrote to him every day because I wanted him to know I was no longer the person he thought I was, so I had to try to reach him before it was too late, and that was the purpose of my open letter to him.

With all of my heart I wanted to be a good father, but I just didn't know how. He was a close to me as my heartbeat, and less than four years he was back on the street and back into the game. After all, he was Big Dave, the man of the hour and sacrificing short term pleasure for long term pain, just like his father. Less than a few weeks he was murdered, shot in the back, two days before his 24th birthday, and I will never forget the words he wrote in one of his last letters he wrote: "Daddy, all of my life, I wanted to be just like you." Every time his words ring in my head my heart literally breaks into a thousand little fragments, how could it not? What happened? What happened, my daughter? How did my yearning to be a father turn out to be so tragic? What happened?

Well, your father is home now, and in 2013, I would enter a world like "Back to the Future," and you would have to introduce me to a technology world that I knew absolutely nothing about. You would have to teach me how to use a cell phone, text, email, and even how to ride the subway, and yes, we would spend an enormous amount of time together. I tried too hard to be the perfect father, but I had to learn that perfection is not a characteristic of human nature. I would make a lot of mistakes and bad judgment, but in the end they only served as a catalyst strengthen* our relationship into what it is today.

I have been blessed to achieve some of life's goals, but none can compete with being a father. Now, I think I got it, my daughter. I think I know what being a father is all about. Every time I hear you call me "Dad" it strikes a cord in my tender heart, and every time you see your father, he wants you to see a reflection of Jesus just as the moon reflects the glory of the sun, for He is the source of my life.

You were there with me when I was baptized on October 20, 2015, and when the Deacon announced, "Will the family of Cheese stand and share with him his baptism?" I saw you leap from your chair, rush to the side of the pool, and recorded your father's baptism on your phone. But it was that look in your eyes and smile upon your face, a look that I don't think I had ever seen before. A look that said to me, "Daddy, I'm so proud of you, and everything is going to be all right."

And so it was on that night, my daughter, your father turned another page, and begin to write the final chapter in his long journey. YES, I'm home at last, and I have found my long lost promised land, and a thousand night I had to die, to one day die no more. So, happy birthday, my daughter!

Love,
Your father

ABOUT THE AUTHOR

DAVID BELTON WAS BORN on September 30, 1944, in South Carolina as the middle child in a family of three. At the age of four, he suffered a stroke leaving him partially paralyzed on his left side. Shortly thereafter, his parent's relationship became turbulent, and eventually he left the family after the birth of his younger brother. His adolescent years were spent in Greensboro, North Carolina. It was there when he dropped out of 9th grade and began a life of petty crime, which landed him a two-year term in a federal training school in Washington, DC (in 1960) for car theft.

David was arrested for several crimes and spent time in three prisons in Lorton, VA. Then, drugs invaded the inner city, and that changed everything. He became a drug dealer and later became addicted in '68, and five years later was arrested for murder in the state of Maryland and was sentenced to life in prison. Prison can be a living hell, but it can also be what one makes it. There, he earned his GED and went on to receive two college degrees. Until his release in 2013, he was the long-term Director of a youth program broadcast on the A&E Network, Beyond Scared Straight, and over the years had the privilege to talk to more than 10,000 youth and young adults.

DAVID BELTON

In addition to his book being published in 1992, he has several published articles to his credit. He is a writer, counselor, youth mentor, and involved in prison ministry. He refused to allow his past to determine his future, and when he was released through the court in 2013, he left better, not bitter.